Table of Contents

Introduction

Wake Up! The War for Your Home (And For Your Future)

Chapter 1: The New Serfdom - Rent, Work, Rinse, Repeat (PG.24)

- The Hidden History of Homeownership
- Serfs and Renters: A Tale of Two Systems
- The Myth of the American Dream: A Renter's Struggle

Chapter 2: Financial Literacy - The Key to Homeownership (PG.56)

- Understanding Your Finances
- Building Credit: The Foundation of Homeownership
- Saving for a Down Payment: Strategies That Work

Chapter 3: Navigating the Housing Market - From Renting to Owning (PG.89)

- Why the Housing Market Is Broken
- Affordable Housing Options: The Truth Behind the Hype
- Finding Your First Home: What You Need to Know

Chapter 4: Financial Assistance and Resources - Don't Leave Money on the Table (PG.116)

- First-Time Homebuyer Programs
- Grants and Loans You Didn't Know You Could Get
- Working with Lenders: How to Get the Best Deal

Chapter 5: The Power of Ownership - Reclaiming Your Freedom (PG.150)

- Homeownership as Financial Freedom
- Breaking the Cycle of Rent
- The Psychological and Social Benefits of Owning Your Home

Chapter 6: Strategic Sacrifice - The Art of Prioritizing Ownership (PG.195)

- Cutting Costs to Save for Your Future
- The Role of Side Hustles in the Homebuying Journey
- Balancing Today's Sacrifices for Tomorrow's Gains

Chapter 7: The Fight for Accessible Homeownership - Reclaiming the American Dream (PG.206)

- The System is Rigged: A Call to Action
- Empowerment Through Ownership
- Creating a Future Where Everyone Can Own

Chapter 8: Real-World Stories of Resilience - From Renters to Homeowners (PG.233)

- Jonah's Story: Breaking Free from the Noise
- Emily's Story: Stability After the Storm
- How Others Are Making Homeownership Possible

Chapter 9: Taking the First Steps Toward Your Future - From Rent to Ownership (PG.280)

- Understanding the Road Ahead
- Building Your Foundation for Homeownership
- Your First Moves in the Housing Market

Conclusion: Your Future Starts Now (PG.312)

- A Guide to Achieving Homeownership
- Making the American Dream Accessible to All

Glossary

Homeownership: The act of owning property, typically a house or condominium, as opposed to renting.

Renting: A temporary arrangement in which a person pays to live in a property owned by someone else.

First-Time Homebuyer: A person who is purchasing a property for the first time, often eligible for special programs or grants.

Down Payment: The initial payment made when buying a property, typically a percentage of the purchase price.

Mortgage: A loan specifically for purchasing property, which is paid back over time with interest.

Private Mortgage Insurance (PMI): Insurance required by lenders when a borrower cannot provide a 20% down payment, typically added to monthly mortgage payments.

Closing Costs: Fees and expenses paid at the closing of a real estate transaction, including things like inspection fees, title insurance, and taxes.

Equity: The value of the homeowner's interest in their property, calculated as the difference between the home's market value and the amount owed on the mortgage.

Amortization: The process of paying off a loan through regular, scheduled payments, with interest and principal amounts.

Appraisal: The process of evaluating the value of a property, typically required before purchasing a home to ensure it is worth the loan amount.

FHA Loan: A loan insured by the Federal Housing Administration, often with lower down requirements and more flexible credit standards.

VA Loan: A loan guaranteed by the U.S. Department of Veterans Affairs, available to current or former military personnel, typically requiring no down payment.

Debt-to-Income Ratio (DTI): A financial measure used by lenders to assess a borrower's ability to repay a loan, calculated by dividing monthly debt payments by monthly income.

Credit Score: A numerical representation of a person's creditworthiness, used by lenders to assess the risk of lending money.

Zoning Laws: Local regulations that determine how properties in certain areas can be used, including residential, commercial, or industrial purposes.

Property Taxes: Taxes assessed by local governments on the value of a property, typically paid annually by homeowners.

Escrow: A financial arrangement in which a third party holds funds for a transaction (such as a home purchase) until all conditions are met.

Closing Date: The final step in the home buying process, when the ownership of the property officially transfers from the seller to the buyer.

Title Insurance: Insurance that protects the buyer and lender against potential disputes over ownership of a property.

Fixed-Rate Mortgage: A mortgage with an interest rate that remains the same for the entire term of the loan.

Adjustable-Rate Mortgage (ARM): A mortgage with an interest rate that may change periodically, based on market conditions.

Subprime Loan: A loan offered to borrowers with less-than-perfect credit, often at higher interest rates to offset the risk.

FICO Score: A type of credit score used by most lenders, ranging from 300 to 850, with higher scores indicating better credit.

Foreclosure: The legal process by which a lender takes ownership of a property when the borrower fails to make mortgage payments.

Refinancing: The process of obtaining a new mortgage to replace an existing one, often to secure a better interest rate or change loan terms.

Grants: Financial assistance provided by the government or nonprofit organizations, often for first-time homebuyers or specific housing needs.

Side Hustle: A secondary job or business that helps supplement a primary income, often used to save for big financial goals like buying a home.

Housing Affordability: The ability of a household to afford to purchase or rent a home, typically measured by the percentage of income spent on housing.

LETS COME TOGETHER

Introduction Into The Modern Divide

Wake up! In today's world, we find ourselves at the precipice of a new kind of class divide—one that isn't merely defined by income but by the ability to access wealth-building opportunities. The wealthiest individuals continue to accumulate vast resources, while many in the middle and lower classes are left behind, struggling to make ends meet. The issue isn't just about stagnant wages; it's about a systemic barrier that prevents large portions of the population from accessing a foundational pillar of financial autonomy: homeownership. As housing prices soar, rents climb, and incomes remain stagnant, more and more individuals are finding themselves locked out of the housing market, unable to secure a path to financial independence.

It's almost like the rich got a head start in a race, and the rest of us are still tying our shoes, tripping over our laces, and hoping we don't fall flat on our faces before the race even starts.

At the heart of this crisis is knowledge inequality—a sneaky, invisible divide that decides who gets to step onto the homeownership ladder and who's stuck holding the "rent" ticket, watching as everyone else climbs. In today's world, owning a home is no longer considered a reasonable goal for most—it's become a VIP club where the entry fee is sky-high, and only the wealthy have the platinum membership. The wealth gap is widening faster than your credit card bill after a weekend shopping spree. If we don't act now, future generations will find themselves stuck in a never-ending loop of unaffordable rents and broken dreams. Sound familiar? You awake now?

Homeownership has always been the gold standard of financial security, stability, and prosperity. For centuries, owning property wasn't just about having four walls and a roof—it was the express ticket to economic freedom, a treasure chest for building wealth, and a legacy that could be passed down like a family heirloom. The best part? It lets you build equity—something renting just can't offer, like trying to fill a cup with water from a leaky faucet. When you rent, you're basically paying someone else's mortgage, growing their wealth while you're left with a pile of rent receipts and no stake in your own future. On the flip side, paying off your own mortgage means you're building wealth, gaining stability, and eventually owning a financial asset that works for you. Plus, as your home appreciates in value, you're securing your future—and not just someone else's retirement fund.

When you rent, you're basically the world's most loyal "temporary" roommate. You foot the bill every month, paying off your landlord's mortgage, and keep the place from falling apart. But in the end, it's the landlord who gets the equity—while you're left with a few empty dinner plates and no dessert. You're the one doing all the work, but they're the ones sitting down to a nice, full plate of financial freedom, while you're left hungry for a future you can't quite taste anything other than boot. Yummy. Do you like that? I didn't think so. Wake up.

Over the last few decades, homeownership has become even more than a financial asset; it has become synonymous with personal success and achievement. The ability to own property was once seen as the dream of individuals working hard to create a better life for themselves and their families, but today, this dream is slipping away for an alarming number of people. The average American has less purchasing power than previous generations, and a growing percentage of the population—especially in urban areas—can no longer afford to buy homes in the markets they live in. This trend is not just an individual crisis; it is a societal problem that threatens to increase economic inequality for generations to come.

We're standing at a critical crossroads. If we don't act now, we'll face a generational divide where the dream of homeownership is reserved for the elite few already perched at the top of the economic ladder. As the gap between the haves and have-nots widens, the climb to financial autonomy will become steeper for those without access to wealth or resources. The wealth generated through homeownership—the rising value of properties, the equity they build, the stability they provide—will stay locked in the hands of a small group. Meanwhile, those without the chance to buy property will be left further behind, stuck renting and building someone else's wealth, not their own.

This isn't just a housing crisis; it's a full-blown social and economic crisis. The inability to afford homeownership isn't just about missing out on a property—it deepens financial instability, limits mobility, and locks entire generations in poverty, making it harder to escape the cycles of inequality. If we let this trend continue, we're on track to create an economically divided society, where the majority remain financially dependent, cut off from the wealth-building opportunities that should be available to everyone. If that doesn't wake you up, I don't know what will. It's time to get moving. You need to get out of bed. NOW.

Let's get one thing straight: homeownership isn't a luxury. It's the damn foundation for financial independence. The minute you own property, you gain the ability to build wealth like nothing else in this country. Let me break it down for you: when you rent, your rent check is just another payment to someone else's bank account. You're helping them build their wealth, not your own. But when you own, every mortgage payment is a step closer to you having something that actually belongs to you.

The key here is equity. For most people, their home is the single most valuable asset they'll ever own. Every dollar you put into your mortgage is building that equity, even if it feels like a long, slow process. You're not just paying for a roof over your head, you're building something that appreciates over time. Over the years, that house will grow in value. If you play it smart, that property could eventually become the cornerstone of your retirement, your children's education, or maybe even another investment. You think you're just paying for a house? No, you're paying for your future.

And here's the kicker: owning a home gives you control. When you rent, you're at the mercy of your landlord—rent increases, lease terms, you name it. They have the power. But when you own, it's your game. You decide if you want to remodel, move, or sell. You decide what the future of your property looks like. That's the freedom of homeownership. That's the kind of control you need to not just survive, but thrive.

This book isn't just about owning a home—it's about taking control of your future, no matter where you come from. Whether you're starting from scratch, fighting through debt, or dealing with barriers the system threw in your way, this is for you. No excuses, no sugarcoating. We're breaking down the real steps to homeownership—without the bullshit. It doesn't matter your income, your background, or your education. The path to ownership is still yours to take, and I'm going to show you how to do it.

We'll explore the history of homeownership and how it's been the key to financial freedom for countless individuals over time. You'll learn how past policies, like the GI Bill and FHA loans, helped millions access homeownership, and how today's government-backed programs and alternative financing options can open doors for you as well. Through real-life stories, you'll hear about individuals who have overcome obstacles to secure their homes, build wealth, and create a better future for their families.

You'll find actionable steps on how to improve your credit, save for a down payment, and access government grants—tools that can put you on the path to ownership. Along the way, we'll emphasize the mental and emotional rewards of ownership, from the sense of pride and security to the ability to invest in your community, all of which contribute to breaking down the walls of economic inequality.

The urgency is real, and the power of homeownership as a tool for building wealth is within your grasp. The question isn't whether you can make it happen—it's how you'll take the first step. WAKE UP!

Thank you

I want to take a moment to express my heartfelt gratitude to everyone who has been part of this journey. To my readers, thank you for trusting me with your time and allowing me to share my experiences and insights. I hope the lessons and stories within these pages inspire you to take bold steps toward homeownership and financial independence. A huge thank you to my family and friends for their unwavering support, and to my fellow veterans who continue to inspire me every day. Your resilience and drive push me to keep advocating for accessible homeownership and equality for all. And of course, thank you to those who believed in the message I wanted to share—together, we can change the narrative and build a more equitable future for everyone.

For those who are ready to take the next step toward homeownership, I'd love to help you on your journey. Whether you're a first-time buyer, a veteran, or someone looking for guidance in a challenging market, I'm here to provide the expertise and support you need. Feel free to reach out to me directly:

Brenton Mann, Realtor
Las Vegas, Nevada
S.200425

Phone: (725) 867-7768
Email: Brenton@realtyvet.com
Website: www.realtyvet.com
Let's work together to turn your dream of homeownership into a reality!

Chapter One

**The Serf's Rebellion:
From Renters to Lords of Our Own
Lands**

Imagine living in a time when land equals power—not just the land you live on but the land that determines your very survival. That was the reality for most people during the feudal era. Owning land was like holding the keys to wealth, security, and status, but for the vast majority? It was a pipe dream, something they could only watch others attain from a distance.

If you were a serf or a peasant, your entire existence was tied to working the land. But here's the kicker—it wasn't even yours. Instead, it belonged to the lords and kings who controlled huge territories and made all the rules. You worked the fields, grew the crops, raised the livestock, but when payday came? The profit went straight into the pockets of the landlord. Your life, your work, your survival—they all depended on land that you had zero claim to.

Imagine this: you're breaking your back from dawn till dusk, keeping the land alive and thriving. But when the reward is due, you're handed nothing but a spot to sleep on land you don't own, under the rule of a landlord who can change the game at any time. No options to buy, no negotiations. If your landlord decides to crank up your rent or demand more work? Tough luck. Sound familiar? The cycle of dependency that trapped serfs back then doesn't feel too far from what renters face today—paying someone else's mortgage with no shot at building their own wealth.

In the feudal system, land wasn't just an asset; it was the ultimate power. Those who owned the land controlled the wealth, dictated who could live there, and laid down the law. The serfs were bound to that land in the same way today's tenants are locked into leases, often paying into someone else's equity with no way out. Things have evolved, sure, but the underlying truth of property as power hasn't budged much.

Now, think about breaking free from that cycle. Imagine trying to own land, gain control, and build your own future, only to find the door slammed shut. You see others accumulating land, wealth, and security, but you're left on the outside, still just trying to get a foothold. That was feudal Europe in a nutshell—homeownership, a shot at building wealth, was a luxury meant for the privileged few. For everyone else, being landless wasn't just an economic issue; it was a denial of freedom.

And what about the lords, the landowners, the kings? They had the ultimate setup. Their land wasn't just a place to live; it was a wealth-generating machine. They reaped the rewards from the labor of peasants, growing their wealth without lifting a finger. This wasn't about fairness or generosity—it was about rigging the economy in their favor. Sound familiar? Today, landlords and corporations enjoy the profits of renter-paid mortgages, while tenants are left with little more than the illusion of stability. The names have changed, but the game remains the same.

And yet, even in that rigid structure, there was one glimmer of hope—a chance for mobility that would eventually come with the Industrial Revolution. As economies evolved and technology advanced, wealth began to flow beyond the grasp of the elite landowners. Skilled laborers, merchants, and entrepreneurs found themselves on a new playing field, one where hard work and innovation could lead to financial independence. The middle class was born, and with it, the dream of ownership.

For the first time, people were no longer bound to the land or reliant on the whims of a landlord. They could earn, save, and—if they played their cards right—own property. This was the start of a new era where ownership could become a stepping stone to social mobility and financial security. It wasn't a free pass, though. Barriers like class, race, and access to education still loomed large, keeping many locked out. But it was a shift, a turning point that hinted at a future where homeownership might be more than just a dream for a privileged few.

It wasn't until after WWII, with policies like the GI Bill, that homeownership really began to take root as an accessible goal for a broader swath of society. These programs opened doors for veterans and their families, allowing them to buy homes, build equity, and establish financial stability—opportunities that had been out of reach for generations. For a time, it seemed like the tide had turned, and homeownership became not just a privilege but an achievable goal for the middle class.

But back in the feudal days? The story was entirely different. If you didn't own land, you had no power, no stability, no wealth to build on. You were stuck, working the land that would never be yours, with no hope of breaking free. Property ownership was as unattainable as royalty for most people. Homeownership, as we envision it today, wasn't even on the horizon.

The legacy of that system still lingers in our modern world. While we've made strides since the days of feudal lords, the disparities created by land ownership persist. The current housing crisis isn't just a problem of high prices; it's an issue of access—who can buy and who's forced to rent. The fundamental reality remains the same: those who can afford to own land are building wealth, and those who can't are paying into someone else's pocket.

Yet the story didn't end in feudal Europe. The Industrial Revolution sparked a transformation, creating pathways for more people to own property. It wasn't an immediate shift, but it was a beginning—a slow, hard-fought evolution toward making homeownership the bedrock of financial security. The opportunities expanded, but so did the challenges.

The Industrial Revolution wasn't just a leap in technology; it was a shift in the entire economic order. Factories rose, industries boomed, and cities thrived. The economy transformed from one rooted in agriculture to one driven by manufacturing and trade. And with this shift came the chance for wealth and, importantly, for ownership. For the first time, the working class and enterprising individuals had a shot at breaking the cycle, at owning land and building a future on their terms. It was the dawn of a new age—one where the power of ownership began to extend beyond the elites. But the road ahead was still long, and the obstacles far from over.

No longer were people bound solely to land for wealth. The factory owners, merchants, and skilled workers began to amass fortunes and, with that wealth, the opportunity to own homes. These individuals weren't born into nobility—they built their wealth by working the system, creating businesses, working in trades, and earning their stake in the new economy. The dream of owning property started to look like a possibility, not a fantasy.

As the middle class began to form, homeownership became more than just a place to live—it became a goal, a symbol of success, and a foundation for financial freedom. The industrial economy opened up avenues for people to accumulate wealth and use that wealth to buy land and homes. For those who had struggled under the feudal system, where land ownership was out of reach, this was a huge step forward.

But while ownership was now more attainable than ever before, it wasn't necessarily easy. The dream of homeownership for the working class was becoming more real, but financial barriers and societal limits still stood in the way for many. Property prices were rising, and securing loans to buy land was a tricky process, especially for those without wealth or access to financial institutions. The idea that anyone could own property was starting to form, but it was still out of reach for many, particularly in growing urban areas.

Despite these barriers, the government began stepping in, with programs aimed at helping more people attain homeownership. After World War II, the GI Bill was introduced, which provided low-interest loans to returning veterans. For many, this was the first opportunity to purchase a home—something that had been nearly impossible before. The GI Bill didn't just help veterans; it helped the middle class grow, by giving families a way to secure a stable future through homeownership.

At the same time, FHA (Federal Housing Administration) loans were also created to help lower-income and first-time buyers purchase homes with lower interest rates and lower down payments. This opened up pathways for people who would have otherwise been shut out of homeownership, especially in the wake of the Great Depression, when financial instability was widespread. These programs helped turn the American Dream of owning a home into a reality for many.

Homeownership began to symbolize more than just a place to live—it became a measure of success. The American Dream was built on the idea that through hard work and perseverance, anyone could own a home, and with that home, build wealth. Owning property wasn't just about having a roof over your head; it was about securing your future, gaining independence, and creating generational wealth. The concept of owning a home as part of the American Dream became inseparable from the ideals of freedom, success, and opportunity.

While the opportunities for ownership expanded, the barriers—like discrimination and economic inequality—were far from eliminated. Not everyone was able to access these programs, and the dream of homeownership still felt out of reach for many groups, particularly marginalized communities.

Despite the progress made after World War II, structural inequalities in housing continued. Government programs that helped white, middle-class families attain homeownership did not always extend those same opportunities to Black families or other minorities due to discriminatory practices like redlining. The promise of homeownership was not equally distributed, and those who were excluded were left to face barriers to entry that lasted for generations.

However, despite these challenges, the rise of the middle class and the expansion of homeownership during this period laid the groundwork for what we know today as the American Dream. Homeownership became, for many, the gateway to financial independence, a tool to build wealth, and a stepping stone to upward mobility—even if it wasn't available to everyone.

As we move into the present day, we find ourselves facing a housing crisis that's as much about access as it is about affordability. The dream of homeownership, once a tangible and attainable goal for millions, is now slipping further out of reach for many Americans. Sure, we've come a long way since the feudal system or even post-World War II, but the divide between homeowners and renters has only grown wider, and it's no longer just about land or property— it's about who has the resources to access them.

The middle class once stood as the beacon of the American Dream—owning a home, building wealth, and creating a stable future. But that dream is increasingly out of reach for many, especially for younger generations burdened by student debt, stagnant wages, and an ever-growing gap between income and housing prices. Homeownership is no longer something everyone can count on as a pathway to stability. In fact, it's becoming a privilege for those who can afford to navigate the labyrinth of rising housing prices, higher interest rates, and a system designed for those already in the game.

This crisis didn't appear overnight. It was decades in the making, fueled by rising property values, stagnant wages, and government policies that, while designed to help, sometimes unintentionally pushed low-income families and minority communities out of the housing market altogether. Over time, the dream of homeownership became increasingly elitist, accessible only to those with the right combination of wealth, credit, and connections.

The path to homeownership, which was once paved with government-backed loans and subsidized mortgages, is now a steep climb for many. Mortgage interest rates have risen steadily, and what was once an affordable monthly payment has now become a barrier to entry. Meanwhile, cities continue to experience rapid gentrification, pushing lower-income families further into the outskirts of cities, where home prices are still somewhat affordable but come with the sacrifice of long commutes and lack of access to vital services. The American Dream of owning a home is increasingly becoming a selective dream, one that is only available to those with substantial financial resources.

If we rewind just a few decades, the housing market in the U.S. looked very different. For much of the 20th century, homeownership was more accessible—but the past 30 years have witnessed an explosive shift in property prices, with many cities seeing prices skyrocket to levels that were once unthinkable. Affordability became the first casualty of this rise, leaving younger generations with fewer opportunities to buy homes. The gap between wages and housing prices has only continued to widen, making it even harder for a single-income household to save enough for a down payment, let alone afford the monthly mortgage payments.

But even more troubling was the inevitable housing crash in 2008. The housing market had been inflated by risky lending practices and the subprime mortgage crisis—a perfect storm where banks issued loans to individuals who could not afford them, leading to widespread defaults and foreclosures. But the real heartbreak of this collapse wasn't just the economic fallout; it was the loss of faith in homeownership as a tool for financial success.

The crash wasn't just an economic disaster—it was a warning. As housing prices reached unsustainable heights, fueled by subprime mortgages and speculative investing, many people found themselves unable to keep up with their mortgages, leading to widespread foreclosures. Homeownership, which had been the symbol of financial success, was suddenly a fragile dream for millions, many of whom lost their homes and were left with nothing.

For those who had been homeowners before the crash, many found themselves underwater, meaning their home was now worth less than the mortgage they owed. The crash destroyed years of hard-earned equity, and the effects were felt for years after. Homeownership was no longer the guaranteed path to wealth it once was. Instead, it became a gamble, one that too many people lost. The aftershocks of the Great Recession continue to ripple through the housing market, making it harder for new buyers to enter the market.

The aftermath of the crash continues to impact the housing market today. The financial dislocation that resulted from the Great Recession pushed the price of homes even further out of reach for the average buyer. Banks tightened their lending standards, making it harder for first-time buyers to secure loans. And while home prices eventually recovered, the recovery was uneven—those who could afford to buy homes already had the means to do so, while millions were left with diminished opportunities. It's as if we learned nothing from the collapse; the same structural inequalities that fueled the bubble still exist today. The wealthy investors continue to snap up properties, while young buyers and low-income families struggle to even enter the race.

At the same time, housing prices continue to climb at a pace far outstripping wage growth. In many cities, the cost of buying a home is now 10 times the average annual income, making it nearly impossible for the average person to afford a home without relying on significant loans or assistance. The dream of homeownership seems more like a distant fantasy for those who don't already have the financial resources to make it happen.

This leaves us with a clear, undeniable truth: homeownership is becoming a luxury reserved for the privileged few. And for the rest of us, the housing market has become another system that's built to keep us locked in place. As more and more people are pushed into the rental market, they find themselves paying someone else's mortgage, with no opportunity to build equity, no stake in their own future, and no means to break the cycle of financial dependency.

This isn't just a housing crisis—it's a social crisis. The inability to afford homeownership is directly tied to a host of larger issues, including economic instability, wealth inequality, and the lack of upward mobility. If this trend continues unchecked, we will see even more people stuck in a system that prevents them from accessing the one tool that's historically allowed people to build wealth: owning property. The question isn't whether homeownership can help break the cycle of inequality; it's whether we can afford to let it slip away from future generations. If we allow it to, we risk deepening the divide and entrenching economic instability for generations to come. This is our moment to act.

The reality is, homeownership has always been a critical step toward financial independence. It's not just about having a roof over your head; it's about the opportunity to build wealth that will grow over time. A home is one of the few assets that appreciates, rather than depreciates. This appreciation allows homeowners to build equity, a financial resource that can be used for future investments, education, or even retirement. However, when homeownership becomes a privilege reserved for a small portion of the population, it leaves the rest of us without the opportunity to use that wealth-building tool, perpetuating cycles of poverty and stagnation.

Imagine what it means for a person's future stability when they are forced to rent rather than own. Renting means paying into someone else's mortgage, building someone else's wealth, and at the end of the day, getting nothing to show for it. Renters never get to see the fruits of their labor beyond a place to live; they don't get the financial security that comes with homeownership. This isn't just about owning a house—it's about owning the future. It's about making sure that the dream of homeownership doesn't disappear entirely for the next generation, and that everyone has a chance to build a future.

Over the past few decades, rental markets have boomed, and with it, the gap between owners and renters has widened. In fact, the rental market has become a profitable industry in its own right, driven by investors who profit from rising rents, while renters continue to fall further into financial insecurity. In many cities, renting has become a long-term cycle for many individuals and families, where the prospect of buying a home is but a distant dream.

As rent increases and homeownership becomes more of a luxury, we have to ask: what kind of society are we building? A society where only the wealthy can access property ownership? A society where generations of people are trapped in financial instability, unable to break out of the cycle of renting without any chance to accumulate wealth? This is a question we need to answer now, because the longer this trend persists, the harder it will be to make homeownership attainable for anyone outside the upper class.

The truth is, we cannot afford to let this trend continue unchecked. If homeownership continues to slip away from the majority of people, we risk creating a society where wealth is concentrated in the hands of a few. Those who already own property will continue to grow their wealth through the appreciation of their homes, while the rest of the population is left behind, watching from the sidelines. The divide will only get wider and more entrenched. And eventually, the dream of owning a home—something that used to be within reach for many—will become as elusive as ever. It will no longer be a stepping stone to financial independence, but a privilege only available to those already in power.

So, the question isn't whether homeownership can help break the cycle of inequality. The question is: how can we ensure that future generations still have the chance to own property, to build wealth, and to change the course of their lives? We can't afford to let homeownership slip away from those who need it most. It's time to put policies in place, advocate for change, and create pathways that allow more people—not fewer—to join the ranks of property owners.

Now is the time to take action. We've seen the past, and we know the impact homeownership has had on the ability of working-class families to build wealth. It's up to us to fight for solutions that make homeownership more accessible, not just for a select few, but for all. We need to advocate for policies that lower the barriers to homeownership, whether it's down payment assistance, more inclusive lending programs, or reforms in zoning laws that can help bring affordable housing to more areas.

More importantly, we need to change the way we think about homeownership in society. It shouldn't be a luxury or a privilege for the wealthy—it should be a right that gives everyone the chance to invest in their future and achieve financial freedom. That starts with understanding the barriers and fighting for the resources and policies that help break them down.

Chapter 2:

Own Or Be Pwned

Homeownership isn't just about owning a house—it's about owning your future. For centuries, property ownership has been a tool for financial security and wealth creation. It's not just a roof over your head; it's an asset that grows over time, giving you equity—a tangible resource you can use for future investments, education, or even retirement. While renting may offer short-term stability, it's homeownership that provides the long-term financial freedom so many of us strive for.

The truth is, when you rent, you're paying someone else's mortgage. Every month, the rent check you write is an investment—not in your future, but in your landlord's. In contrast, when you own a home, that monthly payment is building your equity. It's like paying yourself instead of someone else, because every payment you make brings you closer to owning the property outright. Eventually, that home becomes a financial asset that works for you, not someone else.

Now, I know what you might be thinking: "But the housing market is crazy! How can I afford a home with prices skyrocketing?" Fair point. The barriers to homeownership have never been higher. Rising property prices, stagnant wages, and the difficulty of securing loans are all very real challenges. But even with these obstacles, homeownership remains one of the most powerful tools for financial growth. It's just a matter of knowing where to start and how to navigate these challenges.

Let's break it down: homeownership is a wealth-building machine. Unlike most consumer goods that depreciate over time, property appreciates—it increases in value. As property values rise, so does the equity you've built up in your home. This means that, over time, your home becomes a powerful asset. In fact, research consistently shows that homeownership is the most effective way to build generational wealth.

For millions of people, their homes are their most valuable asset. A home isn't just a place to live; it's an opportunity to invest in your future. Think about it—every dollar spent on mortgage payments isn't just going to keep the lights on; it's an investment that will pay off in the long run, often in the form of increased home equity. This is why homeownership is more than just part of the American Dream—it's part of the wealth-building dream.

Owning a home gives you control—control over your living

situation, control over your finances, and, in many cases, control over your future. While renting means you're at the mercy of your landlord—subject to rent hikes and lease renewals—homeownership means you get to make the rules. You decide how long you stay, how much you pay, and what you do with the property. The security that comes with this control is invaluable, especially as life becomes more unpredictable.

But homeownership is also a lever—it gives you the power to make other financial moves that renting simply doesn't. Whether you choose to borrow against your home's equity to fund a business, send your kids to college, or start investing in other properties, owning a home gives you the ability to leverage your wealth. It's the foundation for creating a financial safety net, whether you want to retire early or pass something down to your children.

There's another, often overlooked, aspect of homeownership that's just as important: stability. When you own a home, you're not just building wealth—you're building a future. Homeownership leads to community investment. Homeowners tend to stay in one place longer, and in turn, they invest in their communities. They build relationships with their neighbors, support local businesses, and contribute to the overall health of the area. Renters, on the other hand, often move more frequently, and while they may still support the community, their sense of investment isn't as deeply rooted.

This is the secret to a stronger society—people who are invested in their homes are more likely to be invested in their communities. Homeownership fosters a sense of pride and belonging, and that sense of stability doesn't just help the individual—it helps the entire neighborhood thrive.

And don't think this is just about making money. Homeownership creates a sense of belonging, a feeling that you're part of something bigger. Whether it's planting your first garden, watching your kids run around in the yard, or just knowing that the house you live in will be your own for years to come, there's something emotionally grounding about owning your home. It's not just an asset; it's a place where memories are made, a place where families grow, and a place where you can truly feel at home.

But this isn't just about you—homeownership is also about legacy. It's about ensuring that your children, and their children, have the same opportunities you had to build wealth, security, and a stable future. By purchasing a home, you're creating an asset that can be passed down through generations, giving your family a head start that most renters simply won't have. Homeownership is the key to breaking cycles of poverty and giving your family the tools they need to thrive.

Now, of course, we're not blind to the fact that homeownership comes with risks. It's not always a smooth ride, and there are challenges—maintaining a home, dealing with unexpected expenses, and managing mortgage payments. But the long-term financial rewards far outweigh the short-term sacrifices. Homeownership isn't without its bumps, but it's worth the ride.

Of course, we're not blind to the fact that homeownership comes with risks. It's not always a smooth ride, and there are challenges—maintaining a home, dealing with unexpected expenses, and managing mortgage payments. While renting may seem like a safer option, it often comes with its own set of hidden costs and frustrations. Rent can increase at the whim of your landlord, and you have no say in the maintenance or upkeep of the property. That leaky faucet? It's someone else's problem, but you're still footing the bill in the form of rent.

Homeownership, however, is about taking control of your financial future. The responsibility of paying your mortgage, fixing that leaky faucet, and mowing the lawn may feel like a burden at times, but it's a burden you control. In exchange for those short-term challenges, you're building long-term wealth and stability that renting simply doesn't offer. Every mortgage payment made is money invested in your future, rather than just another payment that's gone with no return.

But let's not sugarcoat it—homeownership can be costly, especially when you're starting out. There are property taxes, insurance premiums, maintenance costs, and sometimes repairs that come out of nowhere. The key to navigating these challenges is to be prepared. Emergency savings are crucial, as is budgeting for regular maintenance to ensure your home remains an appreciating asset rather than a money pit. Taking care of your home may require effort and investment, but that investment pays off when you build equity and wealth.

Another risk to consider is the housing market itself. While homes generally appreciate in value over time, there are always market fluctuations that can impact home prices. The economic downturns or market crashes, like the one we saw during the 2008 financial crisis, are stark reminders that nothing in real estate is entirely predictable. However, it's essential to note that while short-term market dips can happen, real estate tends to appreciate over time when looked at in the long term. Homeownership is a long-term investment, and if you're planning to stay in your home for several years, the odds are in your favor.

One of the biggest concerns for many is the fear of being "underwater"—owing more on your mortgage than your house is worth. While this fear is valid, the reality is that most homeowners who stay put for the long haul are likely to see the value of their property rise. That's because homes don't just sit still; they appreciate in value over time, especially if you make strategic improvements and take care of them. If you're in it for the long game, the risks become more manageable. The most important thing is to hold onto your property and weather the storms, because homeownership is as much about patience as it is about profits.

And let's not forget about the other challenge: managing debt. For many, buying a home requires taking on a mortgage, and for some, the debt burden can feel overwhelming. Mortgage payments can be hefty, and if you're not careful, you might find yourself struggling to keep up. However, like any debt, the key is strategic planning—understanding your budget, knowing how much you can afford, and sticking to a financial plan. Fixed-rate mortgages are great for this because they offer predictable payments over the long term, providing peace of mind. It's crucial to calculate how much home you can truly afford before jumping in, and ensure that you don't bite off more than you can chew.

That said, homeownership is still worth it. The short-term sacrifices of paying off a mortgage or dealing with home maintenance pale in comparison to the long-term rewards. Think of it this way: you're investing in your future, one mortgage payment at a time. The equity you build, the security you gain, and the legacy you leave for your family—those are things renters can only dream of.

Even when faced with the risks and challenges, the key is not to be deterred. Instead of seeing the bumps along the way as obstacles, think of them as necessary steps in the journey toward wealth, independence, and financial security. Because in the grand scheme of things, those short-term struggles will feel insignificant compared to the financial freedom and stability that comes with owning your own home. Homeownership isn't a one-time win—it's a lifelong investment that pays dividends year after year.

So, as you consider the risks of homeownership, weigh them against the priceless rewards. Yes, it requires effort, patience, and sometimes a little sacrifice. But the opportunity to build lasting wealth, establish a stable future for your family, and create a legacy that spans generations? That's something no renter will ever have. When you own a home, you're not just building wealth—you're building freedom.

The freedom to control your financial future. The freedom to make decisions that affect your long-term stability. The freedom to grow your wealth over time, without being at the mercy of a landlord who can raise rent, change the terms, or ask you to move at any given moment. Homeownership is about empowerment—it's about taking control of your life and ensuring that your future isn't dictated by someone else.

While owning a home may come with risks—like unexpected maintenance costs, fluctuating market values, or the weight of mortgage payments—the long-term rewards far outweigh the challenges. Imagine being a young couple who purchased their first home in the early 2000s. They bought a modest three-bedroom house for $200,000. Fast forward to today, and that same home is now worth over $400,000, thanks to the market's appreciation and the equity they've built. Not only did they gain the security of ownership, but they also built financial stability and wealth for their family in the process. That's the power of homeownership—it grows with you, provides for your future, and rewards your efforts.

Let's not sugarcoat it—homeownership is not always a straight line to success. The housing market is cyclical. Prices rise, then dip. But history has shown that the real value of homeownership comes from the long-term hold. Take the 2008 financial crisis, for example. The housing market crashed, and home values plummeted, leaving many homeowners "underwater" (owing more than their homes were worth). Yet, those who held on—who didn't sell in a panic—saw their properties rebound and appreciate over time. It's a reminder that real estate is a long-term investment. You don't buy a home expecting to flip it in a year or two. You buy it as a future asset, one that appreciates with time.

Another risk is the financial responsibility that comes with homeownership. Owning a home means you're responsible for upkeep, repairs, and unexpected expenses. From roof repairs to plumbing issues, owning a home requires time and money. But here's the thing: each of these investments adds value to your property. Every improvement you make—whether it's remodeling the kitchen or installing energy-efficient windows—is an investment in your future wealth. When you're renting, you're not investing in the property; you're investing in someone else's. With homeownership, every dollar you spend makes your property more valuable and builds equity.

Consider the experience of a couple who bought a home in a gentrifying neighborhood. The neighborhood was a bit rough around the edges, and their house needed some work. But they made the decision to stay, fix up the property, and invest in the area. Ten years later, the neighborhood has transformed, property values have skyrocketed, and their home is now worth three times what they paid for it. The work they put in—both physically and financially—paid off in the form of equity and wealth. The ability to leverage your property—whether through improvements or simply staying the course—can create enormous long-term value.

And let's not forget about the emotional rewards of homeownership. The sense of stability that comes with knowing your home is yours, and no one can kick you out or raise your rent on a whim, is priceless. You have the freedom to paint the walls any color, build a deck, or plant a garden without asking for permission. For many, homeownership is an opportunity to create a space that reflects who they are and what they value. It's a place where memories are made, a space that belongs to you. This emotional investment is just as significant as the financial one.

Consider the psychological difference between renting and owning. When you're a homeowner, you're no longer at the mercy of your landlord's rules. Renting can feel like living in someone else's world. You're constantly adjusting to someone else's needs and expectations. But owning a home means creating your own space—a sanctuary for you and your family. That peace of mind can't be overstated. It's the stability of knowing that no one can tell you to move; it's the sense of pride that comes with making improvements to a place you own.

Homeownership is also an opportunity to leave a legacy. When you own a home, you're not just building wealth for yourself; you're building wealth for your children, your grandchildren, and even generations beyond them. Imagine buying your first home in the 1950s for $20,000. Today, that same property could be worth well over $300,000. If you pass that home down, you're providing future generations with the ability to access a form of wealth-building that was once out of reach. Homeownership isn't just about the present—it's about creating a foundation for the future.

In addition to the tangible benefits of building wealth and creating a legacy, there's a larger social benefit to homeownership. When you own a home, you become invested in your community. Studies have shown that homeowners are more likely to be active in their communities, whether through volunteering, voting, or supporting local businesses. This sense of community investment leads to better neighborhoods, safer streets, and a higher quality of life for everyone. Renters, on the other hand, are often transient, moving from place to place without the same sense of commitment to the area.

The benefits of homeownership are clear, and the risks, though real, are manageable with careful planning and a long-term perspective. Yes, it requires effort, sacrifice, and patience. But the rewards—financial freedom, stability, security, and the ability to build wealth for future generations—are worth the investment. Homeownership is about taking control of your future. It's about building something that lasts—a foundation for yourself and your family to thrive on. While renting may seem like the easier choice in the short term, homeownership is the path to freedom, wealth, and opportunity in the long run.

Homeownership provides the freedom to build something of your own. In today's world, owning a home isn't just a financial decision—it's a personal empowerment decision. The choice to purchase a home can transform your financial trajectory, offering opportunities that renting just can't provide. It's more than just securing a roof over your head; it's about securing your place in the world.

When you rent, you're playing someone else's game. You're subject to rent hikes, rules set by your landlord, and the potential for your living situation to change without notice. On the other hand, when you own, you're building a foundation for your family's future, locking in your costs with a fixed-rate mortgage, and ultimately, giving yourself the freedom to grow. You have the control to make decisions about your property—whether that means remodeling, expanding, or simply making it a home you can pass down.

The wealth that comes from homeownership is often understated. It's not just about how much your home is worth today, but how much it can appreciate over time. A home is an asset that typically grows in value as the years pass. Whether you're buying a single-family home in the suburbs or a condo in the city, if you plan on staying there for a decade or more, there's a good chance your home will appreciate in value, putting you in a position to gain equity. This equity can then be used to fund college, start a business, or even buy additional property.

Renting may feel easier now, but it's a temporary arrangement. Homeownership, in contrast, is a long-term investment in your future, and when that home appreciates in value, it becomes a powerful tool for financial independence.

And then, of course, there's the opportunity that homeownership provides. The opportunity to build wealth through equity, the opportunity to create stability for your family, and the opportunity to achieve financial independence. As rents continue to rise, and as property values continue to increase, the window of opportunity to buy is shrinking. It's easier to get in early—when you start young, when you've got a bit more time on your side, and when the market allows you to make purchases that build long-term financial security. The earlier you make that decision, the more opportunities open up for you. The future may seem uncertain, but homeownership is a bedrock of stability in an ever-changing financial landscape.

As we look ahead, it's crucial to understand that homeownership is a right that needs to be preserved. It's not just about owning a piece of land—it's about keeping the dream of homeownership alive for future generations. Today's housing crisis isn't just an issue of supply and demand; it's an issue of access. The gap between those who own and those who rent is growing wider by the day. In many cities across the U.S., the rising cost of homeownership has put the dream out of reach for many working-class families. The dream of a stable, secure home, in a neighborhood that provides opportunities for growth, seems more distant than ever for younger generations, especially those burdened by student debt and stagnant wages.

But this doesn't have to be the future. Homeownership remains a cornerstone of economic opportunity. It always has been. And with the right tools, resources, and mindset, it can be again. This is why understanding how to overcome the barriers to homeownership is crucial for everyone—not just for financial success, but for maintaining a society where upward mobility remains possible. The next sections will delve into how to achieve that dream of homeownership—from improving credit scores and saving for down payments to utilizing government programs and finding the right financial resources. This journey is entirely possible, and the rewards far outweigh the obstacles.

The path to homeownership isn't just about purchasing a piece of property—it's about securing your financial future. The rewards far outweigh the risks, and while homeownership requires commitment, it provides long-term stability, wealth-building opportunities, and control over your own financial destiny. Every mortgage payment is an investment in yourself, not in someone else's wealth machine. Whether it's growing your equity, creating a legacy, or building a stable foundation for your family, the benefits of owning a home are undeniable.

Yes, homeownership does come with its challenges—unexpected repairs, market fluctuations, and the financial responsibility of managing a mortgage. But in the grand scheme of things, these are small sacrifices compared to the financial freedom and stability it offers in the long run. Unlike renting, where you're just paying someone else's mortgage, homeownership gives you the power to build wealth that can serve you, your family, and even future generations.

The real question is: how do we break through the barriers standing between us and this dream? How do we navigate the rising property prices, the stagnant wages, and the tightening of credit? While the journey to homeownership may seem daunting, the opportunities for success are well within reach with the right tools, guidance, and mindset.

We're standing at a crossroads. The dream of homeownership may feel out of reach for many, but it doesn't have to stay that way. In the next chapters, we'll explore how to overcome the challenges that keep people locked out of the housing market. From improving your credit score to saving for a down payment, from accessing government programs to understanding your financial options—this journey is achievable.

Homeownership remains a cornerstone of financial independence. It's a way to break free from cycles of debt, build lasting wealth, and provide security for your family. And the good news is, you can make it happen. In the chapters ahead, we'll give you the tools to transform that dream into a reality.

Chapter 3:

**A Little Less Sixteen Candles,
A Lot More Rent Hikes**

The dream of homeownership, once within reach for so many, is now slipping away for a growing number of people. What was once a symbol of financial success and security has become an increasingly unattainable goal for millions of Americans, particularly as housing prices continue to soar, wages remain stagnant, and access to affordable loans becomes more difficult. To understand why homeownership is out of reach for so many today, we need to look at the cyclical nature of the housing market. There are times when the market is thriving—homes are being bought and sold at record prices, and property values seem to only go up. But these periods of prosperity often lead to crashes, like the one we saw in 2008. The housing boom, driven by subprime lending and unchecked speculation, eventually gave way to a devastating crash. Many who thought they were building wealth through real estate found themselves upside down on their mortgages, with homes worth less than they owed.

Fast forward to today, and although the market has rebounded in many ways, the underlying issues of price inflation and speculative investing remain. Investors and big corporations are buying up properties, pushing prices even higher and making it harder for regular families to compete. Housing is no longer just a place to live; it's become a commodity—something to buy and sell for profit, while many of us are left trying to keep up.

While we may have left the immediate aftermath of the 2008 housing crash behind, the impact is still being felt today. The tightening of lending standards, a direct result of the subprime mortgage crisis, has made it harder for many first-time buyers to access the financing they need to purchase a home. The recovery from the Great Recession has been slow, and while housing prices have rebounded, wages have not kept pace. This has created a scenario where many potential homeowners are priced out of the market. What used to be an achievable goal is now a distant dream for many, particularly younger generations facing high student debt and a lack of job security. While the housing market was recovering, it was doing so primarily for the wealthy. They had the means to buy property, often with cash or substantial down payments, while many first-time buyers and middle-class families were stuck renting or forced into more affordable areas that offered limited opportunity for financial growth.

Today, the affordability crisis is at an all-time high. In cities across the U.S., home prices have risen to levels that are simply out of reach for many, especially first-time homebuyers. The rise in property values is a direct result of several factors: low housing supply, investor influence, stagnant wages, and rising rents. In many urban areas, there simply aren't enough homes to meet the demand. This has driven up prices and pushed out middle-class buyers who can no longer afford to live in the cities where jobs, schools, and services are located. Large investors and corporate entities have been buying up homes, driving prices higher. These investors are able to pay in cash, outcompeting individual buyers and making it nearly impossible for the average person to secure a home. While wages have remained flat for many working-class families, the gap between what people earn and what they need to earn to afford a home has continued to widen. As wages stagnate and housing prices climb, the dream of owning a home becomes increasingly out of reach.

For those who can't afford to buy, renting is the only option—but rents are rising too. Renters are increasingly finding themselves paying more for less space, without the long-term security that comes with owning a home. As rents rise, many are forced to move further out of the city or to areas with fewer job opportunities, perpetuating the cycle of financial instability. Beyond the financial impact, there are also social implications. When large portions of the population are locked out of the housing market, they lose the opportunity to build wealth and secure their future. The generational wealth that can be created through homeownership is out of reach for many, which means that economic inequality continues to grow. This issue is exacerbated by the fact that homeownership has long been a primary means of accumulating wealth in the U.S. As more people are pushed out of the housing market, the gap between the haves and have-nots widens. Those who own homes benefit from appreciating property values, tax breaks, and the ability to build equity.

Those who rent are stuck paying someone else's mortgage without any hope of building equity for themselves. This is a fundamental issue of economic mobility—if you don't own a home, it's much harder to break free from the cycle of financial instability.

Beyond the financial impact, there are also social implications. Communities with higher rates of homeownership tend to be more stable, with homeowners more likely to stay in one place, build relationships with their neighbors, and invest in the local economy. Renters, on the other hand, are more transient and have less of an investment in the stability of the community. This lack of stability contributes to weaker communities and a decline in the quality of life for everyone involved.

As we move into the present day, it's clear that the affordability crisis has become an entrenched part of the housing landscape. The gap between incomes and home prices has continued to widen, creating a situation where only those with substantial wealth can afford to purchase homes. Young professionals, families with student debt, and individuals with low wages are increasingly locked out of the market. Even those who have stable incomes find it hard to save enough for a down payment while dealing with rising rent costs.

The effects of this crisis are profound and far-reaching. The inability to own a home means that millions of families are deprived of one of the most fundamental tools of wealth-building. Without access to homeownership, financial security becomes harder to achieve, and opportunities for upward mobility become more limited. The lack of affordable housing is leading to a generation that may never experience the same level of financial freedom that previous generations did.

The long-term consequences are not just financial; they're social. As more people are pushed into renting, we risk creating a society where only a small percentage of people own property, while the majority remain renters with no way to build wealth.
Homeownership has long been a path to financial independence, and without

access to it, the divide between the wealthy and the rest of the population will continue to grow.

The longer we let this housing crisis persist, the more people will be locked out of the opportunity to own property. Homeownership isn't just a financial tool—it's a cornerstone of stability, independence, and wealth-building. If we don't address the barriers to homeownership, we risk creating a future where only the wealthy can own property, and the rest of society remains locked in a cycle of renting and financial dependency. This isn't just a housing crisis—it's a social and economic crisis. The inability to afford homeownership will only increase financial instability, reduce mobility, and entrench poverty, making it increasingly difficult for individuals to break free from systemic cycles of inequality.

Homeownership isn't just a financial tool—it's the foundation for building generational wealth, creating stability, and securing independence for yourself and your family. In the next chapters, we'll look at how we can start breaking down these barriers. From government programs to financial strategies, there are ways to navigate the current housing market and turn homeownership into a reality for more people. The fight for homeownership isn't just about purchasing a house—it's about securing a financial future for yourself, your family, and generations to come.

As the affordability gap continues to widen, we must recognize that the issue isn't just about rising prices—it's about the changing nature of our economy and the lack of opportunities for homeownership for many people. For decades, property ownership has been one of the most reliable ways to build generational wealth. But now, with fewer people able to afford homes, we're witnessing a dangerous trend: a growing portion of society that is permanently renting without any hope of achieving the financial independence that comes with owning property.

One of the most troubling aspects of this crisis is the role that large institutional investors play in driving up housing prices. They've found real estate to be a lucrative investment, buying up properties in bulk, outbidding first-time buyers, and effectively locking many would-be homeowners out of the market. This isn't just a minor trend—it's a systemic shift that's making it harder for regular families to access homeownership. These investors don't have the same limitations as everyday buyers. They often have cash on hand, and with that financial leverage, they can pay top dollar, making it difficult for the average person to even get a foot in the door.

Imagine a young couple, looking to buy their first home. They've saved for years, working hard to put together a down payment, only to find that homes in their price range are being bought by big companies who see these properties as opportunities for profit. They're unable to compete with the cash offers or the quick deals that investors are making, and their dream of homeownership starts to fade away. This is the reality for millions of people today.

Moreover, even if you can afford to buy a home, the challenges don't stop there. The cost of living in many parts of the country has skyrocketed, and the financial burden of purchasing and maintaining a home can be overwhelming. Property taxes, homeowners insurance, and maintenance costs quickly add up. What was once an achievable dream of stability and independence can turn into a financial burden if not managed carefully. However, despite these challenges, the benefits of homeownership remain undeniable.

We can't ignore the role that government policies have played in shaping the housing market. After the 2008 financial crisis, the government stepped in with a variety of programs aimed at stabilizing the market and helping people achieve homeownership. Yet, while these programs were helpful in some ways, they also created an uneven playing field. The recovery from the crash was not equally distributed—some people had access to affordable loans and financial assistance, while others were left behind. The wealthiest buyers, for instance, were able to scoop up properties at a discount during the downturn, while working-class families were stuck waiting for the market to recover.

Today, we're still feeling the aftereffects of these policies. The housing market has bounced back, but it has come at a cost. Prices have gone up, and wages have failed to keep up with these increases. While homeownership used to be a way for working-class families to build wealth, it has now become an impossible dream for many.

We also can't overlook the broader economic implications of this crisis. The inability to afford homeownership perpetuates inequality, not just financially, but socially. Renters, especially those stuck in expensive, overcrowded areas, face immense challenges. They may struggle to save for the future, build credit, or invest in their own education or careers. Homeownership, on the other hand, provides the foundation for individuals to secure their future, build equity, and pass down wealth to future generations. When people are locked out of homeownership, they lose the ability to build long-term wealth, and this has long-term consequences for their families, their communities, and society as a whole.

In urban centers, especially, the demand for affordable housing is far outpacing the supply. The cost of housing in cities like New York, San Francisco, and Los Angeles has skyrocketed, and many people are finding themselves unable to live in the cities where they work, shop, and play. They are being pushed further out to the suburbs or rural areas, where housing is more affordable but where job opportunities are fewer, and public services are harder to come by. This not only makes it more difficult for these individuals to build their lives, but it also separates people from the economic hubs they need to be part of to succeed.

It's a paradox: in a time when the demand for housing is at an all-time high, the prices keep climbing, and the availability of affordable homes is shrinking. The dream of homeownership, which has been part of the American Dream for so long, is becoming an unattainable luxury. With wages not rising to meet the demands of an inflated market, fewer people are able to secure loans, and those who do find themselves paying more than they should for less-than-ideal properties.

It's not just an economic issue—it's a social issue as well. A society where only the wealthy can afford homeownership creates a stark divide between the haves and have-nots. It leads to a world where the poor stay poor and the rich get richer, as those with property can ride the waves of market appreciation, while those without are left struggling to keep up with ever-increasing rent payments. In many ways, this growing divide is a ticking time bomb for social unrest, as the vast majority of people continue to be shut out of the wealth-building opportunities that property ownership provides.

This is why the crisis in housing affordability is more than just an economic issue—it's a matter of fairness, access, and opportunity. We must find ways to bridge this gap and make homeownership a possibility for more people. If we don't, we risk perpetuating a system that limits the economic mobility of millions of people, condemning them to a life of financial insecurity and limiting their opportunities for success.

It is time to recognize that homeownership is not just a luxury—it's a fundamental right. But it is a right that is being denied to too many people. The current state of the housing market is unsustainable. The barriers to homeownership are simply too high for too many people, and the dream of owning a home is becoming a distant memory. But we cannot let that happen. It's time to take action.

We need to advocate for policies that will make homeownership more accessible to everyone—not just the wealthy, but the middle class, working families, and future generations. There are solutions out there, whether through government programs, financial education, or changes to zoning laws. By working together, we can create a future where homeownership is no longer a privilege reserved for the rich, but a right for all. It is not just an economic issue; it's a social issue as well. A society where only the wealthy can afford homeownership creates a stark divide between the haves and have-nots. It leads to a world where the poor stay poor and the rich get richer, as those with property can ride the waves of market appreciation, while those without are left struggling to keep up with ever-increasing rent payments. This growing divide is a ticking time bomb for social unrest, and if left unaddressed, it threatens the very fabric of our society.

The dream of homeownership, once seen as the universal key to financial independence, is slipping further out of reach for many Americans. This isn't just a financial crisis—it's a moral one. A right that was once accessible to working-class families is now a privilege for the wealthiest, and the consequences are felt throughout society.

Without homeownership, families are locked out of the wealth-building process that has defined the American Dream. A rental system that benefits landlords but leaves tenants financially adrift exacerbates wealth inequality. Renters are caught in a never-ending cycle, paying off someone else's mortgage without ever gaining any equity in return. The lack of access to homeownership forces entire generations into financial limbo—dependent on rising rents, unable to save, and unable to invest in their futures.

The housing market today is not just about buying and selling homes. It has become a hyper-competitive, profit-driven landscape. With institutional investors sweeping up properties, the idea of a home as a place for personal growth and stability is being replaced by the concept of a home as a commodity to be bought and sold for profit. The real estate market, once the realm of individual buyers, has become a space where the rich continue to amass wealth and the rest of society struggles to keep up.

But this doesn't have to be the way it continues. The rising tide of homeownership inequality isn't inevitable—it is the result of a series of policies, decisions, and market forces that can be changed. We can reverse this crisis. By focusing on affordable housing initiatives, expanding financial literacy programs, and making policy reforms, we can reclaim homeownership as an achievable goal for the majority, not just the few.

The rising tide of homeownership inequality isn't inevitable—it is the result of a series of policies, decisions, and market forces that can be changed. We can reverse this crisis. By focusing on affordable housing initiatives, expanding financial literacy programs, and making policy reforms, we can reclaim homeownership as an achievable goal for the majority, not just the few.

Homeownership is more than just a financial strategy. It's about security.

It's about taking back control over your future, your finances, and your home. It's about breaking the cycle of renting, and, ultimately, it's about making sure the American Dream remains a possibility for everyone, not just the wealthy few.

The opportunity to own a home and build wealth shouldn't be a privilege—it should be a right. It's time to ensure that future generations don't inherit a broken system but are equipped with the tools to thrive in a society where ownership is accessible, achievable, and sustainable.

Chapter 4:

Not Your Fathers Future of Homeownership

Owning a home isn't just about putting a roof over your head—it's about securing a stake in your future. It's about building wealth, creating stability, and gaining control in a world where everything else seems to be up for grabs. But as the economic divide grows, the question isn't just who can buy a home, but who can keep one. The American Dream of homeownership, once a widely accessible goal, is inching closer to a privilege for the few, not the many. If we want that door to stay open, it'll take some serious recalibration of how we think, act, and legislate.

This shift isn't happening in isolation. The rising cost of homes, combined with stagnant wages, inflation, and increasingly stringent lending standards, has made it harder for people to buy. And for those who do manage to buy, the pressure to keep up with payments in a market this volatile is relentless. Homeownership, long seen as a stepping stone to security, has become a fragile tightrope walk. If we're serious about preserving it as a realistic goal, it's time to view homeownership as a broader societal investment, with benefits that extend far beyond individual prosperity.

In many ways, the challenge of homeownership today mirrors the economic divide of past centuries. We've come full circle—from the feudal age when land equaled power, through the industrial boom that opened up property ownership to the middle class, to today, where owning property feels increasingly out of reach again. Back then, it was the lords and kings who held all the cards. Today, it's corporations and investors gobbling up properties, turning neighborhoods into rental empires and leaving everyday people priced out. The freedom and opportunity that comes with homeownership shouldn't be a relic of the past, but without intervention, that's exactly where it's headed.

To carve a path forward, we need to recognize that homeownership is more than just a personal financial decision; it's the foundation for a thriving society. Stable homeownership builds communities, creates local engagement, and offers a means of financial resilience that renting simply doesn't provide. When individuals own homes, they have a vested interest in the neighborhoods they're part of—schools improve, crime rates drop, and people invest more in their surroundings. But when only a select few can afford to buy, the ripple effects of ownership dry up, and communities suffer.

There's no quick fix, but history offers some insights. After WWII, for example, programs like the GI Bill and FHA loans opened doors for millions to buy homes, creating the backbone of America's middle class. These policies didn't just put roofs over heads; they enabled people to build wealth and pass it down to future generations. However, access to these benefits wasn't universal, and many groups were left out, including Black families and other marginalized communities. This lack of access has left scars that are still visible in today's racial wealth gap. Learning from these successes and failures can guide us toward creating more inclusive, modern solutions that genuinely serve everyone.

One approach to ensuring a more accessible path to homeownership is policy reform focused on affordability. This means zoning laws that allow for more affordable housing to be built, especially in high-demand urban areas. It also means examining the role of corporations in the housing market. When corporations buy up properties en masse, they drive up prices and reduce availability, especially for first-time buyers. Instituting restrictions on bulk property purchases or offering tax incentives to individuals over corporations could help shift the balance back toward those looking to buy a primary residence, not just another investment.

At the same time, we need to rethink lending practices. Mortgage lenders still heavily favor high credit scores and large down payments, which leaves out vast segments of the population, especially young people and those burdened by student debt. Expanding access to low-interest loans, down payment assistance, and flexible mortgage programs can bridge that gap, enabling more people to break into the housing market. For instance, government-backed loan programs that prioritize first-time buyers or those with lower credit scores could be game-changers for making homeownership more inclusive.

Educational initiatives also have a key role to play. Financial literacy—teaching people about budgeting, saving, and managing debt—can empower potential homeowners to make informed decisions. It's a long-term strategy but a necessary one. Understanding how to save for a down payment, manage a mortgage, and handle property taxes can mean the difference between successful homeownership and foreclosure. Schools, nonprofits, and employers all have a role to play in making financial literacy accessible.

Moreover, we need to consider new, creative ownership models. The traditional single-family home with a white picket fence isn't the only pathway to building wealth through property. Co-buying, where friends or family members jointly purchase a property, can help more people enter the market. Community land trusts, where residents collectively own land and share equity, provide another avenue. Models like these can open doors for people who might otherwise be shut out of traditional homeownership.

In a similar vein, expanding access to rental-to-own programs could be transformative. These programs allow tenants to gradually build equity in a property, with their rent payments contributing toward eventual ownership. While not a widespread solution, rental-to-own can be a powerful tool for those who lack the upfront cash for a down payment. It gives renters a direct path to ownership, providing stability and a chance to invest in their futures.

Another promising area for change is the promotion of green housing incentives. As climate change becomes a more pressing concern, there's an opportunity to tie sustainability and affordability together. Offering tax breaks or low-interest loans for energy-efficient homes, solar panels, and sustainable building materials not only makes homeownership more accessible but also reduces long-term costs for owners. By building affordable, eco-friendly homes, we're not only helping people buy houses but also protecting the planet and future generations.

While these strategies are crucial, we also need to shift our cultural perspective on renting. For many, renting is no longer a temporary phase but a long-term reality. Policies that protect renters—like rent control, tenant rights, and eviction protections—are essential for creating stability. But even more than that, we need to consider how to make renting a financially viable option for building wealth. This might mean offering renters opportunities to invest in the properties they live in or providing tax incentives for long-term renters. Rethinking the role of renting in wealth-building can help level the playing field for those unable to buy.

As we push for these changes, it's essential to recognize that the housing crisis isn't just about policy or money—it's about values. If we see homeownership as a fundamental right and not a privilege, we're more likely to create systems that prioritize people over profits. The wealthiest among us should not have exclusive access to stability and security; these are universal needs. Ownership offers a degree of freedom, control, and resilience that renting doesn't, and if we're serious about giving everyone a fair shot at financial freedom, we need to start treating housing as a human right, not just an economic asset.

Looking ahead, it's clear that making homeownership accessible to future generations won't happen without collaboration across the board. It's going to take lawmakers willing to enact tough policies, developers committed to building affordable housing, and communities willing to support sustainable development. We can't afford to wait for the market to "correct" itself because, as history shows, the market often works best for those who already have a leg up.

The stakes are high, and the window of opportunity is narrowing. As more of the housing stock gets bought up by investors and as prices continue to rise, future generations will find it increasingly difficult to break into the market. But with thoughtful policies, inclusive financial systems, and a commitment to housing as a right, not a privilege, we can turn the tide. We've seen how access to ownership transformed lives in the past, and there's no reason it can't do the same now—if we're willing to make it a priority.

Ultimately, this isn't just about buying a home; it's about buying a future. The ability to build wealth, create stability, and invest in one's community should be within everyone's reach, not just those with financial privilege. Homeownership can and should be a tool for economic mobility, a foundation for building a better life. But achieving that vision requires us to ask tough questions, make difficult changes, and above all, recognize the intrinsic value of giving everyone a stake in the places they call home.

The American Dream of homeownership has been a beacon for

generations, but it's time to update what that dream means. It's not just about individual success but about creating a society where everyone has the chance to succeed. Housing isn't just another asset class to be traded and profited from—it's the backbone of our communities and the launchpad for financial independence. For everyone's sake, we need to ensure that future generations have the same opportunities for stability and growth that their predecessors enjoyed.

When we talk about creating a future where homeownership is within reach for everyone, it's essential to recognize that the tools and policies that worked in the past may need a refresh for today's challenges. The GI Bill, FHA loans, and other post-WWII measures were groundbreaking in their time, but today's economic landscape looks very different. Housing prices have outpaced wage growth, the cost of living has soared, and younger generations are weighed down by student debt and other financial burdens that weren't as prevalent in previous decades. Given these realities, it's clear that we need to think creatively to develop new pathways to ownership.

For starters, we need to take a hard look at housing inventory. In many high-demand areas, there simply aren't enough homes to go around, which drives up prices and pushes potential buyers out of the market. To address this, local governments can adopt policies that encourage the construction of affordable housing. This could include zoning reforms to allow for higher-density housing in urban areas, incentives for developers to build lower-cost units, and tax breaks for properties that meet certain affordability criteria. By making it easier to build, we can increase supply and make homeownership more attainable for more people.

Another powerful tool in expanding access to ownership is down payment assistance programs. A major hurdle for first-time buyers is saving for a down payment, especially as property prices climb higher. Programs that provide grants or low-interest loans for down payments can help bridge this gap. These programs could be funded by federal or state governments, or even through partnerships with private companies that have a vested interest in creating stable, community-rooted workforces. Down payment assistance isn't a silver bullet, but it can be a critical step in making ownership more accessible for younger buyers or those without generational wealth to fall back on.

Additionally, we need to confront the issue of rising interest rates. When rates are high, monthly mortgage payments become harder to afford, pricing out potential buyers. While the Federal Reserve's interest rate decisions are beyond our direct control, we can explore alternative mortgage products that offer flexibility. For example, adjustable-rate mortgages (ARMs) or graduated payment loans, when structured responsibly, could provide lower initial payments that gradually increase over time, allowing buyers to ease into ownership as their income grows. Programs that cap interest rates for first-time buyers or those in underserved communities could also provide relief.

One area often overlooked in the homeownership discussion is the role of credit. Credit scores are crucial in determining eligibility for a mortgage, but the traditional credit scoring system can be a significant barrier for those who don't fit the mold. Many people—especially younger individuals and immigrants—have thin or nontraditional credit histories, making it harder for them to qualify for a loan even if they're financially responsible.

Creating alternative credit models that consider rental history, utility payments, and other indicators of reliability could help level the playing field. Several fintech companies are already exploring this, but to make a real impact, these models need broader adoption by traditional lenders.

It's also worth considering the potential of community-driven ownership models. For example, community land trusts (CLTs) allow individuals to purchase homes while the land itself remains owned by a nonprofit organization dedicated to affordable housing. This reduces the cost of buying and keeps housing prices stable over the long term, as the land remains community-owned and cannot be sold off for profit. CLTs have been successful in several U.S. cities, offering a promising blueprint for other regions facing housing affordability challenges. By giving communities a direct stake in the housing market, CLTs not only create affordable homes but also foster stronger local ties and shared responsibility.

Another avenue to explore is expanding access to co-buying arrangements. Co-buying—where two or more people pool resources to purchase a property—can be an effective way to share costs and make homeownership achievable for those who might not afford it individually. While co-buying may not fit the traditional image of homeownership, it's a model that suits modern realities, especially as multi-generational living and friend cohabitation become more common. Legal frameworks that clarify rights, responsibilities, and exit strategies for co-buyers could help make this option more mainstream and accessible.

Tax policy also plays a crucial role in shaping the housing market, and reforms here could make a real difference. For example, offering tax deductions for renters similar to the mortgage interest deduction available to homeowners could help renters build savings toward a down payment. Additionally, adjusting capital gains taxes on home sales to be more favorable for first-time or low-income sellers could incentivize long-term homeowners to downsize, freeing up larger homes for families looking to buy.

Finally, we need to talk about education. Financial literacy—specifically around home buying, mortgages, and property management—is a vital piece of the puzzle. Many prospective homeowners aren't fully aware of the responsibilities and potential pitfalls of owning property, leading to stress and financial hardship down the line. By integrating homeownership education into high school curriculums, community workshops, and even employer-sponsored programs, we can prepare people for the realities of buying and owning a home. Knowledge is power, and informed buyers are better equipped to make sustainable choices that benefit themselves and their communities.

As we look to the future, one thing is clear: preserving homeownership as a realistic option for the majority will require more than just minor adjustments. It will demand a collective effort—policymakers, financial institutions, developers, and communities all working together to create a system that values people over profits. Homeownership, in its best form, isn't just about individual wealth; it's about stability, investment in community, and the promise of upward mobility.

The goal isn't to turn everyone into a homeowner, but rather to ensure that those who aspire to own have a fair shot at achieving that dream. We have the tools and resources to make this happen; it's simply a matter of priority. With intentional policies, innovative financing, and a commitment to inclusivity, we can create a housing market that serves everyone—not just those at the top.

Let's take a step back and recognize that, in many ways, the housing crisis reflects deeper, systemic challenges within our society. If we genuinely want to preserve homeownership as a path to financial independence and community stability, we need to rethink how housing fits within our broader economic priorities.

One critical shift we can make is to redefine success in housing policy. For too long, the focus has been on metrics like market growth, property values, and returns on investment. But what if we redefined success to prioritize stability, accessibility, and affordability? By reorienting our metrics, policymakers could better align housing goals with the needs of everyday people rather than catering to speculative investors or profit-driven developers. Imagine a future where success is measured not by how high property values soar but by how many families achieve stable housing they can afford.

Furthermore, we can't ignore the role that big money plays in the housing market. As large investment firms and institutional buyers snap up residential properties, they drive up prices, making it harder for individual buyers to compete. Regulating corporate ownership of single-family homes, or creating tax penalties for companies that hoard residential properties, could slow this trend. These policies wouldn't eliminate corporate buying entirely but could create a more balanced market where individuals and families have a fair chance.

In addition, governments could implement land use policies that actively support affordable housing projects over luxury developments. Too often, high-end apartments and condos receive priority because they promise higher returns, while affordable units get sidelined. By offering incentives for affordable housing and penalizing projects that don't meet these needs, cities could shift the focus from profits to people. This approach has been effective in places like Vienna, where affordable public housing makes up a significant portion of the market, offering a model for other cities to follow.

It's also essential to address zoning laws, which often restrict affordable housing options by limiting the types of buildings that can be constructed in certain areas. Exclusionary zoning, which reserves large swathes of land for single-family homes only, exacerbates housing shortages and drives up prices. By reforming these zoning laws to allow for mixed-use and multi-family developments, cities can open up new pathways for affordable housing without needing to expand geographically.

Beyond policy, fostering a culture that values and supports homeownership can make a significant impact. Imagine if community organizations, local businesses, and schools collaborated to create programs that promote homeownership as a communal goal rather than an individual achievement. For instance, a "Homeownership Savings Match" initiative, funded through partnerships between local governments and employers, could offer matching funds for people saving toward a down payment. This kind of program could encourage people to set and achieve their homeownership goals, knowing they have community support along the way.

Education, too, is critical here. We often assume people understand the complexities of the housing market, but buying a home is one of the most significant financial decisions a person can make—and yet, it's rarely taught. Making financial literacy a priority, especially in high schools and community programs, would help prepare the next generation of homeowners. Additionally, expanding these educational efforts to include knowledge about taxes, maintenance, and the long-term responsibilities of homeownership would make homeownership more sustainable for first-time buyers, reducing foreclosure rates and fostering stable communities.

We should also explore innovative models like "rent-to-own" programs, which give renters an option to build equity as they make monthly payments.

In these programs, a portion of the rent goes toward the purchase price of the home, allowing renters to accumulate equity over time. This approach offers a more gradual entry into ownership, reducing the need for a large upfront down payment. Programs like this have been successful in some areas, providing a valuable middle ground between renting and traditional home buying. Expanding access to these programs, particularly in areas where home prices are high, could help bridge the gap for many who otherwise couldn't afford to buy.

Finally, it's crucial to acknowledge that homeownership, while valuable, may not be the goal for everyone. Some people prefer the flexibility of renting, especially in today's economy, where job mobility can be essential. Rather than viewing renting as a failure to achieve the American Dream, we can frame it as a valid choice with its own benefits. Policies could be developed to offer renters security, such as stronger protections against eviction, rent stabilization measures, and access to savings programs. This approach can provide financial stability for renters while keeping the door to homeownership open if their goals change.

Ultimately, preserving homeownership as a viable pathway to wealth and stability requires collective effort. It's not simply about making a few policy tweaks or expecting the market to adjust on its own; it's about reimagining a housing system that works for everyone. By working together, we can build a future where ownership is attainable for all, regardless of background, income, or zip code.

Homeownership has the power to transform lives, providing security, community investment, and the chance to build a legacy. But to unlock this potential, we need a system that prioritizes people over profits, that values stability over speculation, and that offers fair access to the dream of ownership. This vision is within our reach, but it requires commitment, creativity, and, most importantly, the belief that homeownership isn't just a luxury for the fortunate—it's a foundation for a better future for everyone. Homeownership has long represented more than a financial milestone; it's a stake in community, a step toward security, and a chance to shape a legacy. As we look forward, it's crucial to remember that the dream of ownership isn't just a personal ambition but a cornerstone for societal resilience. By reimagining our housing policies, fostering innovation, and championing accessibility, we can make homeownership a path open to everyone, not just the privileged few. The foundation is set, and the tools are within reach—it's up to us to build a future where the right to own a home is as attainable as the dream itself.

Chapter 5:

**I Ain't Learnen So Gooood :
Education In Crisis**

I chime in with haven't you people ever heard of... opening a God Damn Book? No? In a world where knowledge can mean the difference between poverty and prosperity, financial literacy has always been a cornerstone of power—yet, historically, it's been a privilege reserved for the few. Imagine a time when understanding wealth was less about complex investment strategies and more about knowing how to navigate basic finances: saving, managing debt, or even simply keeping track of spending. For much of history, though, this knowledge was kept out of reach for the working class, hidden behind the walls of exclusive institutions and private tutors reserved for the wealthy elite.

For centuries, those in power understood that keeping financial knowledge scarce was a way to maintain control. In medieval Europe, the nobility held land and wealth, while peasants and serfs were tied to their estates, with little understanding of economic management. The very concept of "financial literacy" would have been meaningless to them—yet their labor fueled the economy. Landlords benefited from a lack of economic mobility among their laborers, who were bound to their roles without the tools to envision a life beyond them.

This pattern persisted into later eras, even as societies evolved. As economies grew and industrialized, wealth became more accessible, but the means to manage it did not. For the rising working class in the Industrial Revolution, wages were higher than ever before, but understanding how to save, invest, or even budget was not part of the picture. Without access to financial education, the working class often remained in a cycle of dependency and instability, with money slipping through their fingers as quickly as it was earned.

It wasn't just about access, either. Literacy itself was a barrier for much of history, with formal education limited to those who could afford it. The ability to read contracts, understand interest rates, or keep financial records was a skill denied to large portions of the population. This gap kept wealth concentrated among those who already had it, passing financial skills—and, therefore, financial security—down through generations. Knowledge became an inheritance of its own, shaping wealth disparities that we still see today.

As the working class expanded, some philanthropic efforts sought to bridge the gap. Early financial literacy campaigns emerged from progressive movements that believed education was a pathway to independence. But these efforts were small and often treated as a side note to other social reforms, failing to reach the people who needed them most. And as economies became increasingly complex, so did the tools of wealth, from mortgages and credit systems to investments and retirement plans. For those without financial education, these systems often became traps instead of tools, locking them into cycles of debt and dependency.

Without an understanding of how to navigate the financial systems, people remained vulnerable to exploitation. In many ways, the lack of financial literacy reinforced class divides, creating a population that could work for money but was ill-equipped to make that money work for them. Even when the doors to wealth seemed to open, as they did with the rise of the middle class, they were often only slightly ajar, and without the knowledge to push them open, many were left looking in from the outside.

By the early 20th century, financial products were beginning to target everyday people, from installment plans for goods to the first home loans. But without an understanding of interest rates or debt repayment, many of these offerings became financial pitfalls. Debt and credit systems expanded access to goods and homes, but they also exposed the economically vulnerable to new risks. Financial literacy could have served as a shield, but for most, it remained elusive.

The historical lack of financial education created a legacy that's still with us. Today, many people inherit a knowledge gap, where managing finances is learned through trial and error—often costly and painful. As we move forward, bridging this gap is critical not only for individuals but for society at large. Economic empowerment through knowledge isn't just a personal asset; it's a public good.

The 20th century brought seismic shifts in both society and the economy. As economies grew more complex, the need for financial literacy became evident to reformers and social activists who saw knowledge as a tool for equality. Financial literacy began to be viewed as a key to breaking cycles of poverty, granting individuals not just the chance to earn money, but the understanding to manage it effectively.

Early financial literacy movements were often rooted in the work of community leaders, nonprofits, and philanthropic organizations. Reformers began to recognize that without education, the growing availability of consumer credit, mortgages, and new financial products could easily lead people into debt. Campaigns to teach budgeting, saving, and debt management began cropping up in urban centers, where the rising working class struggled to navigate this new financial landscape.

One notable movement came in the form of settlement houses in American cities, where volunteers offered classes in budgeting, household management, and even basic banking. These centers aimed to equip immigrants and low-income families with skills to better manage their finances, understanding that knowledge was a pathway to stability. Educators focused on empowering individuals to make informed financial decisions, breaking down complex topics into practical lessons.

As financial products became more diverse, so too did the need for deeper financial understanding. By the mid-20th century, schools began incorporating basic economic principles into their curriculums, recognizing that children needed to be taught early about money management. However, these efforts were patchy, often only available in wealthier districts or as part of optional programs. The promise of widespread financial education remained largely unfulfilled, with gaps persisting, especially in low-income areas.

In the 1960s and 70s, the financial literacy movement gained new momentum with the rise of social reform initiatives. Grassroots organizations began advocating for the financial rights of underprivileged communities, emphasizing the need for widespread access to credit and fair lending practices. They recognized that financial literacy was essential in combating predatory lending practices that disproportionately affected minority communities. Organizations like the NAACP and the Urban League began offering financial education programs, linking economic empowerment with civil rights.

The financial literacy movement grew more mainstream in the late 20th century, as the consumer credit industry expanded and homeownership became a central pillar of the American Dream. With credit cards, car loans, and mortgages becoming standard, the average household was managing more complex finances than ever before. Nonprofits, banks, and community groups saw the need for financial education as both a social responsibility and a business necessity, recognizing that financially literate customers were less likely to default or face financial distress.

However, despite these efforts, financial education often fell short of reaching those who needed it most. Many programs were underfunded or localized, unable to achieve the scale needed to have a nationwide impact. The rise of the internet in the late 1990s and early 2000s brought new opportunities for accessible financial literacy, yet digital divides meant that not everyone could benefit equally. The promise of financial empowerment remained incomplete, as financial literacy failed to become a universally accessible resource.

Today, the legacy of these early movements is visible in the continued work of financial literacy nonprofits, public school programs, and online resources. Yet, despite all the progress, there remains a deep need for accessible financial education that reaches across socioeconomic boundaries. As the economy evolves, so too must our approach to financial literacy, recognizing it as an essential life skill that everyone deserves.

With these foundations, the importance of financial literacy as a tool for empowerment has become clear. In the next section, we'll explore how today's buyers can leverage financial literacy to navigate modern challenges in homeownership, especially as they face obstacles that previous generations never encountered.

In the modern financial landscape, homeownership is no longer just about saving for a down payment and securing a mortgage—it's about navigating a complex web of credit scores, debt-to-income ratios, fluctuating interest rates, and housing market volatility. As the barriers to entry grow, financial literacy becomes an even more essential tool for potential buyers, giving them the knowledge and confidence to approach the housing market with realistic expectations and clear strategies.

For today's prospective homeowners, especially younger generations burdened with student debt, stagnant wages, and rising living costs, the path to homeownership can seem daunting. Financial literacy isn't a luxury; it's a necessity. Understanding how to budget effectively, manage credit, and build savings for a down payment can mean the difference between achieving the dream of homeownership and being permanently priced out of the market.

First-time buyers often face a learning curve when it comes to credit management, which plays a critical role in the mortgage approval process. Many potential homeowners aren't fully aware of how credit scores impact interest rates and loan terms, or they may not understand how to improve their scores. This lack of knowledge can create barriers that might otherwise be avoidable. For instance, someone with a good income but a limited credit history may struggle to qualify for a traditional mortgage. But with the right financial guidance, they could explore options like FHA loans, which are designed for buyers with less established credit.

Moreover, managing debt is another critical skill for today's buyers. With rising levels of student loans and credit card debt, maintaining a healthy debt-to-income ratio is essential for mortgage qualification. Financial literacy programs that teach debt management and consolidation strategies can empower buyers to approach their finances more effectively, opening doors that may have otherwise remained shut. Prospective homeowners who understand how to balance debt while building savings are better positioned to make a solid case to lenders.

Another layer of financial literacy that's crucial in today's housing market is understanding the true cost of homeownership. Unlike renting, owning a home comes with additional expenses beyond the monthly mortgage payment, including property taxes, homeowner's insurance, maintenance costs, and potential homeowners association (HOA) fees. These are often overlooked by first-time buyers who may not realize the long-term financial commitment required to maintain a property. Programs that emphasize total cost planning help buyers prepare for these realities, reducing the risk of financial strain down the line.

Today, potential homeowners also benefit from understanding the nuances of mortgage products. Not all loans are created equal, and financial literacy can equip buyers to choose between fixed-rate, adjustable-rate, and interest-only mortgages based on their financial situation and future plans. A buyer who understands these options is better able to select a mortgage that aligns with their budget and goals, rather than feeling pressured into a decision that might not be sustainable in the long run.

Financial literacy also includes preparing for the inevitable ups and downs of the economy. Markets fluctuate, and home values can rise or fall depending on economic conditions. Buyers who are financially educated understand that real estate is a long-term investment, and they're less likely to panic during economic downturns or housing market corrections. Instead, they can approach homeownership with a sense of resilience, knowing that over time, the benefits of owning property often outweigh short-term fluctuations.

In a rapidly changing financial environment, knowledge is power. Financial literacy doesn't just prepare today's buyers for homeownership; it empowers them to make sound decisions that can build wealth and stability. With the right foundation, buyers can feel confident navigating the housing market, understanding their options, and taking control of their financial futures.

As traditional homeownership becomes less attainable for many, creative and alternative ownership models are emerging as powerful solutions. These models, like co-buying, community land trusts, and rent-to-own arrangements, offer new pathways to building equity and stability in ways that align with today's economic realities. For many aspiring homeowners, these alternatives present viable options that bridge the gap between renting and traditional buying, making homeownership accessible to those who might otherwise be excluded.

Co-buying, where friends, family members, or even strangers come together to purchase property, is becoming increasingly popular. By pooling resources, co-buyers can afford properties they couldn't individually, enabling them to build equity without taking on unsustainable debt. This model reflects the shifting dynamics of modern life, where multi-generational households and shared living arrangements are more common. For young people saddled with student debt, or for families seeking to support aging relatives, co-buying offers a flexible and financially feasible route to homeownership.

Legal frameworks for co-buying are evolving to provide clarity and protection for all parties involved. Agreements can outline ownership shares, define responsibilities for upkeep, and establish protocols for selling or buying out another's share if circumstances change. This structure not only provides security but also reduces the risk of disputes, making co-buying a more sustainable option. As housing prices continue to climb, co-buying offers a path that turns an individual struggle into a shared opportunity.

Community land trusts (CLTs) offer another promising approach. In a CLT, a nonprofit organization owns the land and sells the homes on it at affordable prices, allowing individuals to buy homes without bearing the full cost of land ownership. Homeowners can build equity, but the trust retains ownership of the land, keeping housing affordable for future buyers. This model has been successful in cities like Boston and New York, where housing prices are especially high. By maintaining long-term affordability, CLTs create stability within communities, preventing displacement and encouraging local investment.

The benefits of community land trusts go beyond financial access. Because CLTs are managed by community members, they often foster a sense of collective responsibility and pride. Residents have a voice in decision-making, which strengthens the social fabric of the community. For many, CLTs represent more than a home; they are a means of preserving neighborhood identity and resisting the forces of gentrification that can drive longtime residents out. This community-centered approach offers a model that balances individual ownership with collective well-being.

Rent-to-own programs also provide a viable pathway to ownership for those who can't afford a traditional down payment. In these arrangements, a portion of the monthly rent goes toward purchasing the property, allowing renters to build equity over time. This structure gives tenants a clear path to ownership, offering the stability of homeownership without the immediate financial hurdle.
Rent-to-own arrangements are especially valuable in high-cost areas where saving for a down payment can

take years. By turning rent payments into an investment, these programs offer a tangible sense of progress for those working toward owning a home.

Rent-to-own programs can be particularly empowering for individuals who might not qualify for traditional mortgages due to limited credit histories or lower income levels. By allowing tenants to gradually build ownership, these programs create a stepping stone to financial independence. For many renters, knowing that their payments are contributing toward future ownership adds a layer of security and motivation, transforming what would otherwise be a recurring expense into a long-term investment.

In addition to these models, emerging forms of shared equity housing are also gaining traction. Shared equity models, such as limited-equity cooperatives, allow buyers to purchase homes at below-market rates in exchange for sharing a portion of the property's future appreciation. This arrangement makes ownership more affordable while still offering the potential for wealth-building. These cooperatives often come with built-in support systems, such as maintenance teams or financial advisors, which help members navigate the responsibilities of homeownership.

These innovative models demonstrate that homeownership doesn't have to follow a one-size-fits-all approach. By expanding the definition of ownership to include collective and gradual pathways, we can create a housing market that meets the needs of a diverse population. Co-buying, community land trusts, rent-to-own programs, and shared equity housing all offer viable alternatives to traditional ownership, making it possible for more people to invest in their futures.

As housing costs rise and economic pressures increase, these models offer a glimpse into what the future of homeownership could look like: inclusive, flexible, and resilient. The idea that owning a home must be a solitary pursuit is outdated. Today's economic realities call for solutions that bring people together, that redefine ownership as a shared journey rather than an individual achievement. By embracing these new models, we can make the dream of homeownership accessible to a broader and more diverse population, strengthening communities in the process.

While innovative ownership models provide a range of options, systemic policy reforms are essential for making homeownership accessible on a broad scale. Without supportive policies, even the most promising models can only address part of the problem. Policies that promote affordability, prevent exploitation, and encourage inclusive practices are crucial to creating a housing market that serves everyone—not just those with existing wealth or favorable circumstances.

One major area for reform is zoning. In many cities, zoning laws restrict housing density, limiting the availability of affordable homes in high-demand areas. By loosening these restrictions and allowing for higher-density developments, cities can increase the housing supply and make homeownership more attainable. For instance, permitting duplexes, triplexes, or accessory dwelling units (ADUs) in single-family neighborhoods can create a greater variety of housing options and price points, making it easier for first-time buyers and low- to moderate-income families to find affordable homes.

Incentivizing the construction of affordable housing is another powerful tool. Governments can offer tax breaks, grants, or low-interest loans to developers who prioritize affordable units in their projects. By rewarding the creation of affordable housing, policymakers can make it financially attractive for developers to contribute to a balanced housing market. Some cities have implemented inclusionary zoning policies that require developers to set aside a certain percentage of units in new buildings for affordable housing, helping to maintain economic diversity within communities.

Limiting corporate ownership of residential properties can also play a crucial role in creating a fairer housing market. When investment firms and large corporations buy up single-family homes and apartment complexes, they reduce the supply of homes available to individual buyers and drive up prices. Policies that restrict bulk purchases by corporations or impose additional taxes on investment properties can level the playing field for everyday buyers. By curbing corporate influence in the housing market, we can help ensure that housing remains a tool for individual wealth-building rather than merely another asset class for profit.

Mortgage reform is also essential to expanding homeownership access. Traditional mortgage requirements—such as high credit scores and large down payments—can exclude responsible, financially capable individuals who don't fit the standard criteria. Expanding access to government-backed loans, creating flexible mortgage products, and supporting alternative credit models can open doors for aspiring homeowners. Policies that recognize rental history, utility payments, and other nontraditional indicators of financial responsibility can make mortgages more accessible to a broader demographic, particularly young people and immigrants who may lack conventional credit histories.

Down payment assistance programs represent another impactful policy tool. For many prospective homeowners, saving for a down payment is one of the biggest obstacles to buying a home. By providing grants, low-interest loans, or matched savings programs, governments and nonprofits can help bridge this gap. Down payment assistance programs not only reduce the initial financial hurdle but also give buyers a sense of stability and confidence as they embark on homeownership. These programs can be especially valuable in high-cost areas, where even modest homes require substantial upfront investment.

Rental-to-own policies and initiatives also warrant greater support. Rent-to-own arrangements allow tenants to gradually build equity in a property, creating a clear path to ownership. By encouraging landlords and property management companies to offer rent-to-own options, policymakers can provide renters with an attainable path to homeownership. Rent-to-own agreements can be structured with transparent terms that prioritize the tenant's right to purchase, ensuring that renters have a genuine opportunity to transition from leasing to owning.

Equitable tax policies can further support aspiring homeowners. While homeowners benefit from mortgage interest deductions, renters don't receive comparable tax incentives for their housing expenses. By offering tax deductions or credits for renters, governments can help renters save more toward a future down payment. Additionally, revising capital gains tax laws to favor long-term homeowners—particularly those in low- and middle-income brackets—could encourage stability in the housing market and make it easier for individuals to build equity over time.

Moreover, housing policy should prioritize community land trusts (CLTs) and other shared ownership models. Supporting CLTs through funding, tax incentives, or legal protections can empower more communities to establish these trusts, preserving affordability and preventing displacement. As we discussed earlier, CLTs allow people to own homes without the full cost of land ownership, which can be transformative in high-cost areas. By investing in CLTs, governments can foster stable, resilient communities where residents have a stake in both their properties and their neighborhoods.

These policy reforms, while varied, share a common goal: to make homeownership accessible and sustainable for all. As the housing market grows increasingly competitive, these reforms offer practical solutions to counter rising costs and reduce barriers. Each policy initiative addresses a different aspect of the housing crisis, from affordability and equity to accessibility and stability. Implemented together, they can create a housing ecosystem that serves everyone, ensuring that the dream of homeownership remains within reach.

But policies alone aren't enough. To truly democratize homeownership, we need a collective shift in how we view housing and its role in society. Moving forward, we must see housing not only as an asset but as a right—a foundation for stability, community, and economic security. With thoughtful reforms, we can build a housing market that reflects these values and prioritizes people over profit.

If we're going to build a society where homeownership is a realistic goal for all, we have to look beyond quick fixes. Real change will come when we prioritize housing as a societal good, a foundation upon which communities can thrive, and not merely a commodity for profit. This means rethinking our values, committing to systemic reforms, and fostering a culture that sees homeownership as integral to a stable and prosperous society.

Imagine a future where aspiring homeowners aren't limited by arbitrary barriers or the financial whims of a speculative market. In this future, policies align to make homeownership accessible to a wide range of people, from young professionals and single parents to immigrants and middle-income earners. It's a future where no one has to choose between a roof over their head and financial security, where renting is a valid choice but not the only one available to those outside the top economic tiers.

In this vision, communities play an active role in supporting homeownership, not just through government initiatives but through localized efforts. Neighborhood groups, nonprofits, and employers partner to provide financial literacy programs, homebuyer workshops, and down payment assistance. Local banks offer flexible mortgage products that adapt to people's changing financial realities, making it possible for more people to become homeowners without overextending themselves.

These communities also recognize that a diverse housing market strengthens the social fabric. Homeownership isn't limited to single-family houses; it includes co-ops, townhouses, condos, and multi-family units that suit different lifestyles and financial situations. By embracing these varied paths to ownership, we break free from the one-size-fits-all model and open the door to more equitable, accessible housing options. And for those who continue renting, protections are in place to ensure stability and financial growth opportunities, keeping the dream of ownership within reach.

Education will play a critical role in sustaining this future. Financial literacy programs start early, preparing students with the knowledge and tools they need to make sound financial decisions. Schools, community organizations, and employers work together to ensure that financial education isn't just a luxury for the privileged but a core part of every person's education. By understanding budgeting, mortgages, credit management, and long-term planning, the next generation enters adulthood equipped to take on homeownership with confidence and foresight.

Alongside education, sustainable housing initiatives become mainstream. Affordable housing and eco-friendly homes aren't mutually exclusive. In our envisioned future, green housing incentives encourage the construction of energy-efficient homes accessible to all. These homes offer long-term savings on utility costs, reduce environmental impact, and contribute to healthier communities. Tax credits and low-interest loans make green retrofitting affordable for existing homeowners, allowing them to invest in their properties without facing prohibitive upfront costs.

As we reimagine homeownership, we must also confront the realities of economic disparity. Affordable housing isn't just a moral imperative; it's an economic necessity for a balanced, stable society. When more people can own homes, they contribute to the local economy, pay taxes, and invest in their neighborhoods. This positive feedback loop creates stronger communities, more vibrant local businesses, and better public resources, benefiting everyone—not just homeowners.

Achieving this vision of homeownership won't be easy, and it won't happen overnight. It requires a long-term commitment from policymakers, communities, and individuals to continuously adapt and innovate. We must remain vigilant against policies that prioritize profit over people and challenge practices that lock certain groups out of the market. By fostering a culture that values stability, inclusivity, and community investment, we create a housing landscape that truly serves everyone.

This is the future we must strive for—a future where homeownership remains a powerful means of building wealth, independence, and community. When we view housing as a right, not a privilege, we lay the foundation for a more equitable society. This isn't about taking away from one group to give to another; it's about leveling the playing field so that everyone has the chance to achieve financial security through property ownership.

In closing, preserving the dream of homeownership is more than an economic goal; it's a commitment to a society where everyone has the opportunity to secure their place, invest in their future, and feel rooted in their community. The road to this future will require bold action, inclusive policies, and a relentless focus on making homeownership accessible. But with these steps, we can ensure that the dream of homeownership—along with its promise of stability, growth, and community—remains within reach for all.

Chapter 6:

Time to Act – Building a Future Where Ownership is for Everyone

Let's face it: the dream of owning a home is getting harder to reach, and if we keep going the way we are, it's only going to get tougher. This isn't just a trend or a temporary setback—it's a call for change, a signal that we need to rethink what we want our society to look like. We're talking about more than just property or money here. We're talking about a vision where owning a home isn't just for the privileged few, but for anyone willing to work for it. It's a future where stability, security, and opportunity don't get auctioned off to the highest bidder but are made accessible to every person, every family, every community.

So how do we get there? It starts with each of us realizing that this isn't someone else's problem. The solutions we need won't come from waiting on market forces to "correct themselves" or hoping that housing prices will magically drop. They'll come from collective action, community-driven movements, and a mindset that homeownership isn't just an individual achievement, but a societal investment. In this chapter, we're diving into what it means to stand up for accessible homeownership, from practical steps individuals can take to the larger systemic shifts we should be demanding. This is your call to action.

One of the first steps in making homeownership a reality is taking control of your own financial journey. Nobody's going to do this part for you, and in a world where knowledge often gets hoarded by those already in the know, it's up to each of us to close that gap ourselves. This means building financial literacy, understanding credit, saving with intention, and being strategic about spending. These might sound like simple things, but they're game-changers.

Get familiar with your financial standing—know your credit score, understand your debt-to-income ratio, and build a budget that prioritizes saving. Look for free or low-cost financial literacy courses in your community, and use online tools to track your progress. Remember, this isn't just about ticking boxes; it's about arming yourself with the skills to face a market that doesn't play fair. And while it might feel like a drop in the bucket, financial confidence is the first line of defense in an increasingly exclusive housing market.

Here's the truth: personal finance can only take you so far. No amount of budgeting or saving will make up for policies that favor corporations over individuals, or that allow entire neighborhoods to be snapped up by investors. That's why we need to push for housing policies that put people first. Think about rent controls, tax incentives for individual buyers, or restrictions on corporate ownership of single-family homes. These are policies that can start leveling the playing field, and they're policies that need public backing.

Get involved in local advocacy, attend city council meetings, and support candidates who prioritize affordable housing. When you see a policy proposal on the table, ask yourself who benefits—and if the answer is wealthy investors or big corporations, speak up.

Your voice matters here. Individual actions are powerful, but combined, they create the kind of pressure that gets results. Demand housing policies that prioritize community stability over profit margins.

Communities have power, and one of the biggest myths out there is that change only happens from the top down. In reality, some of the most effective solutions come from communities working together, pooling resources, and setting their own terms. Community land trusts, cooperative housing models, and neighborhood-based financial workshops are just a few examples of local initiatives that make ownership more accessible. These solutions aren't just about housing—they're about building networks of support that keep communities strong and affordable.

If you're in a community that values homeownership, start the conversation. Reach out to neighbors, local nonprofits, or advocacy groups to explore options like land trusts or housing cooperatives. Get people talking about co-buying options or support systems for first-time buyers. These may not be traditional paths to ownership, but they're effective, and they keep resources local. In a world where communities are increasingly bought and sold by outsiders, grassroots solutions put ownership back in the hands of the people who live there.

Ownership doesn't have to mean a white picket fence or a 30-year mortgage. We need to start embracing alternative ownership models like co-buying, rent-to-own arrangements, and shared equity housing without the stigma. For too long, there's been this idea that if you're not buying outright, you're somehow settling or taking a lesser path. But these alternative models are smart, sustainable, and practical solutions to an unaffordable market. They allow people to build equity, gain stability, and establish roots without the traditional upfront costs.

Spread the word about these options. Talk to friends, family, and colleagues. Share success stories, connect people to resources, and push back on the myth that there's only one way to own a home. As more people understand the flexibility and potential of alternative models, we can create a culture where these paths are not just accepted but encouraged as valid ways to achieve homeownership.

For a lot of people, renting isn't a choice; it's a necessity. But the fact that it's sometimes viewed as "falling short" of homeownership only adds to the pressure and stigma surrounding housing. Let's rethink this narrative. Renting can be a practical, even strategic, decision, and it doesn't mean the door to ownership is permanently closed. Just as importantly, we should be advocating for renters' rights, protections, and even programs that allow renters to build wealth and stability.

Whether you're a renter or a homeowner, stand up for policies that protect tenants—rent control, anti-eviction laws, and tenant rights are all essential. Push for programs that allow renters to invest in the properties they live in, or for tax incentives that help renters build savings toward a down payment. When we stop viewing renting as second-best, we start creating a housing market that respects everyone's needs, regardless of their buying power.

At the heart of this call to action is a mindset shift: housing shouldn't be a commodity to be traded, speculated on, or hoarded. Housing is a basic need, a human right, and the foundation of a healthy society. When we see it this way, the solutions become clearer. We stop accepting that it's normal for a few to profit at the expense of many, and we start building systems that prioritize people over profits.

Advocate for this mindset. Whether it's in conversations with family, social media posts, or at public meetings, make it clear that you believe housing should serve communities, not corporations. The more people who adopt this view, the closer we get to making it a reality. Ownership is about security, stability, and dignity—and that's something everyone deserves

Chapter 7:

**Strike Back The Empire:
Take Ownership of Your Future**

Imagine a future where owning a home becomes as rare as spotting Bigfoot. Homeownership, once the gold standard of security, is now a distant dream for most—a privilege reserved for those who can afford to buy on a whim while the rest of us are left holding leases and eviction notices. Sound far-fetched? Maybe. But as housing prices skyrocket and wages stand still, that future isn't as far off as we'd like to think. If we don't start fighting for it now, homeownership could be one more item on the list of "things we took for granted"—right up there with affordable healthcare and cheap coffee.

For generations, homeownership has been more than just having a roof over your head. It's been a ticket to stability, a way to grow wealth, and a source of pride. It's what allowed our grandparents to work hard, buy homes, and build a little something to pass on. But in today's market? The idea that we might do the same feels like a cosmic joke. Every year, the barriers get higher, and every month, it feels like we're one paycheck away from being swallowed whole by the rent cycle.

This isn't just an individual crisis—it's a societal one. When people can't afford to buy homes, entire communities lose out. When homeownership slips from our grasp, we lose more than property; we lose power, autonomy, and any real say in the places we live. That means no equity, no stable investment, and certainly no picket fence. We're stuck helping landlords build wealth while we collect receipts and fight off the creeping sense that we're running on a hamster wheel that someone else set to 'max speed.'

Here's the bottom line: homeownership is worth fighting for. It's not just a personal asset—it's a public good, the foundation of thriving communities. Owning a home keeps people grounded, gives them a vested interest in the future of their neighborhoods, and creates stability for generations to come. If we don't stand up now and push back against the barriers keeping people out, we risk watching the power of ownership slip away, right into the pockets of people who see property as nothing more than an investment to flip and forget.

Owning a home is more than just a place to sleep at night. It's a statement—a stand against living under someone else's roof, playing by someone else's rules, and paying into someone else's mortgage. For decades, homeownership has given people the freedom to build their lives on their terms. Want to paint the walls bright yellow? Go ahead. Plant a garden, knock down a wall, put up a fence—it's your call. That's the magic of ownership: control. But with the cost of housing spiraling out of reach, that control is starting to feel like a relic from a time when wages could actually keep up with the price of a modest home.

The truth is, homeownership isn't just about a house. It's about freedom from the rent trap—a cycle that's designed to keep people moving from one apartment to the next, one year-long lease after another, without ever getting a stake in the ground. Rent is, at its core, a never-ending ticket to someone else's profit. The landlord collects, the bank appreciates, and you're left with empty pockets and zero equity. It's a system built to keep the keys to stability in someone else's hands, while you're left holding nothing but a lease renewal and a higher rent bill.

But the ripple effects of lost ownership run even deeper. Think about community ties. When people own their homes, they're more likely to care about what happens to their neighbors, their schools, their local businesses. They're invested, literally and figuratively, in keeping their community safe and thriving. Renters, on the other hand, are often left on the sidelines, constantly wondering if they'll be priced out when the next lease renewal hits. When you don't know if you'll still be around in a year, it's hard to plant roots.

Homeownership is what gives us the power to be more than temporary residents. It allows us to anchor ourselves, to push for changes in our communities, and to fight for what's right because we have a stake in it. It's the difference between watching things happen around you and being able to influence them. Without that foundation, we're all just passing through, paying rent for a view of someone else's dream.

Now, here's the kicker—preserving homeownership isn't just about individual wealth or personal pride. It's about pushing back against a system that increasingly treats housing as a profit machine rather than a basic human right. Every time we lose ground in the fight for accessible ownership, we lose a bit of that autonomy, that ability to say, "This is mine. This is my corner of the world, and I'm not going anywhere."

The funny thing is, it's not like we're asking for luxury here. Nobody's out there demanding a mansion with a private beach and a butler to answer the door. All people want is a shot at something solid—something that belongs to them, that doesn't get pulled out from under them every time the market gets hungry for more profits. But the way things are going, you'd think we were asking for the moon.

In reality, it's not just homeowners who benefit from this kind of stability. When people own, neighborhoods get stronger. Schools get better. Local businesses get a boost. Crime rates drop. It's a classic case of what benefits one ultimately benefits everyone. And yet, despite all this, the path to homeownership keeps getting narrower, like some exclusive club that keeps raising its entry fee while looking down its nose at everyone on the outside. It's like they've forgotten that owning a home used to be the ultimate sign that you'd made it—not because you got lucky or knew the right people, but because you put in the work, saved up, and finally got a place to call your own.

But maybe that's the point. Maybe the whole system is set up to make homeownership feel like an impossible dream so that when you do make it, you're supposed to feel grateful just to be there. Meanwhile, the rest of us are left watching from the sidelines, clutching our leases and wondering if we'll ever get off the rental treadmill. It's a system that's stacked from top to bottom, built to make sure that those who already have keep on getting, while the rest of us just keep on paying.

It's easy to feel like the deck is stacked too high, like there's no way to break through. But that's exactly why this fight matters. Because if we just sit back and let this happen, we're letting them rewrite the rules on who gets to own a piece of the future. We're handing over the keys to a system that decides for us who's allowed to build wealth, to put down roots, to feel secure. And every year we don't push back, that dream slips further out of reach.

So, where does that leave us? It leaves us with a choice. Either we stand by and let the cost of ownership climb until it's out of sight for most, or we start making noise. We start treating homeownership like the cornerstone of freedom that it is—something worth fighting for, not just for ourselves, but for everyone who comes after us. We rally for policies that make ownership accessible, we demand fairer lending practices, and we push back against the corporations that would turn every neighborhood into their own personal piggy bank. We don't need a million-dollar home. We just need a fair shot at owning the four walls we live in.

Breaking out of the rental mindset isn't just about wanting something different; it's about making a conscious decision to stop paying for someone else's investment and start building your own. Decide today that renting, while sometimes necessary, isn't the endgame. Owning a home means investing in your future, not padding someone else's portfolio. Make that commitment to yourself—no more feeding the rental beast forever. It's time to turn your money into something that actually grows for you.

Start by getting clear on why homeownership matters to you. It's not just about having a place to call your own—it's about stability, freedom, and the chance to build real wealth. Maybe it's the idea of a space you can truly make your own or the financial security that comes with building equity. Hold onto that reason, because there'll be challenges ahead, and knowing your "why" will keep you moving forward when the journey gets tough.

To take control of this journey, you have to get real about where you stand financially. Look at your income, your spending, and, yes, even your debt. No need for guilt or shame—this is just information, a starting point. Track your spending for a month, break down where your money goes, and look for places where you can cut back and save. It's amazing how just seeing the numbers can shift your perspective, helping you feel more in control and ready to make a change.

Then, start building a habit of saving—even if it's a small amount to start. If you can only put aside $20 a week, that's okay. The point isn't about hitting big numbers right away; it's about building a habit. Set up a separate account for your homeownership fund and keep it out of sight, out of mind. Every dollar saved is one step closer to getting the keys to your own place, and over time, those small contributions will add up.

One of the most crucial pieces of this puzzle is credit. A good credit score can be the difference between getting a manageable mortgage and being stuck in a high-interest trap. Start by paying bills on time, keeping credit card balances low, and avoiding new debt if possible. If you've faced credit challenges, consider a secured credit card to rebuild your score. It's not glamorous work, but the impact is real—and it could save you thousands when it's time to get a loan.

Next, set a realistic down payment goal. Don't get stuck thinking you need 20% down—yes, it's ideal, but there are plenty of loan options for buyers who don't have that much. Look into FHA, VA, or USDA loans if you qualify. These programs are designed to make homeownership more accessible, and understanding your options will help you set a down payment goal that feels achievable rather than overwhelming.

Educate yourself on mortgages, even if the terms sound complicated at first. The basics are manageable, and knowing how loans work—fixed-rate, adjustable-rate, interest—will help you feel more empowered in the process. Knowledge here can literally save you thousands, so invest the time. Seek out resources from trusted places like the Consumer Financial Protection Bureau or HUD to help you grasp the essentials.

And don't wait until you feel "ready" to talk to a mortgage professional. Mortgage brokers can give you a clear idea of what you'll need to qualify and guide you on your next steps. It's like getting a roadmap from someone who's navigated the route many times before. Even if ownership is a year or two away, early advice can set you up for a smoother journey.

As you plan, picture what kind of home would work for you. It doesn't have to be your dream mansion—just a place that's truly yours. Maybe it's a two-bedroom condo in a neighborhood you like or a starter home with a yard. Visualize it, and let that vision guide you. Knowing what you're aiming for can keep you motivated when saving feels tough or the journey seems long.

Finally, stay focused, but be flexible. The path to ownership isn't a straight line, and markets, life, and financial situations can all throw you curveballs. But that doesn't mean you're not getting there. Every dollar saved, every point on your credit score, and every bit of knowledge gained is a step closer. This isn't a sprint—it's a steady climb, one that builds resilience along the way.

So let's make ownership a priority, not just a possibility. Shifting from renting to owning isn't just a financial journey; it's a decision to prioritize your future and build something real for yourself. Start today, with small steps and steady progress. Because every effort you put in is bringing you closer to a place you can finally call your own.

As you go through this process, remind yourself that setbacks don't mean failure. Maybe an unexpected expense slows down your savings or your credit score isn't improving as fast as you hoped. That's all part of the journey. Don't let these moments knock you off track—instead, see them as building resilience along the way. Each hurdle you overcome is a step closer to financial independence. Owning a home isn't just about crossing a finish line; it's about creating a foundation that you can stand on, no matter what life throws your way.

Keeping a long-term view is critical here, even if the short-term sacrifices sometimes sting. This journey isn't about getting everything right from day one; it's about staying in the game, moving forward—even if it's inch by inch. Because every small step is a brick in the structure of your future stability, a future where the choices benefit you, not just your landlord's bottom line.

Embrace the process and remember that your journey to homeownership is more than a transaction. It's a way of stepping into the driver's seat of your own life, creating the financial security and autonomy that renting simply can't offer. Each dollar saved, each budget reviewed, each plan you make toward owning a home is an investment not just in a property, but in yourself. This journey is about more than getting a roof over your head; it's about reclaiming control, building your stability, and designing a life where your hard work truly works for you.

When the road feels long, remind yourself that you're working toward something that will pay you back in ways renting never will. Homeownership gives you an equity stake in your future, a lasting foundation for building wealth, and a sense of pride that comes from knowing you're investing in something real. This isn't just about beating the system—it's about building a life where you're free from the limitations of the rental mindset, where you can finally say, "This is mine."

Now, think about what you can do today. Start by finding one area where you can cut back and put those savings toward your goal. Or make it a point to check your credit score regularly and celebrate the small wins along the way. Treat each decision as a step forward, a vote of confidence in the life you're building. It may take time, but with every step, you're proving that this dream is worth fighting for.

It's time to wake up. For too long, the system has been stacked in favor of the few at the expense of the many, with a financial playbook that leaves the average person stuck in cycles of rent, debt, and dependency.

Homeownership, once a cornerstone of stability and freedom, has become a privilege for those who already have a head start. Meanwhile, the rest of us are footing the bill for someone else's empire, giving our hard-earned cash to landlords and investors who profit off our need for shelter. The reality is brutal, but here's the truth: you can fight back.

Owning a home isn't just a financial choice—it's a form of protest. It's a way to say "no" to a system designed to keep you locked out, paying into someone else's wealth while your dreams stay on hold. Homeownership gives you the one thing renting never will: real control. It's your chance to step off the treadmill of rent increases and restrictions, to claim a space that's yours in a world that's all too willing to sell it out from under you.

Think back to the legacy of ownership throughout history, from the feudal lords who hoarded land to keep peasants tied to their fields, to the industrial barons who built their fortunes on the backs of workers with no stake in their own futures. The fight for homeownership has always been about more than land—it's been about self-determination, about creating a path to stability and wealth that doesn't rely on the whims of the powerful. And yet, here we are, with new lords in the form of corporate investors and landlords, carving up neighborhoods and keeping the rest of us renters, tenants, outsiders.

Remember how the middle class once rose, brick by brick, thanks to programs like the GI Bill and FHA loans, opening the doors to homeownership for millions of Americans. For a brief time, homeownership became a real possibility for the average family, a ticket to financial security and independence. But over time, the system shifted again, favoring big money and leaving many first-time buyers scrambling against rising prices and restrictive policies. Now, more than ever, homeownership is a battleground, and securing a home means reclaiming your power in a world where wealth is too often reserved for the elite.

Every dollar you put toward owning your own home is a step away from the rental trap. Every payment on your mortgage is a protest against a system that's happy to keep you paying rent, lining pockets that aren't your own. Owning your home means building equity for yourself, investing in something real and lasting, while the rental cycle just keeps you treading water, working hard but never getting anywhere. This isn't just about housing—it's about breaking out of a system designed to keep you financially dependent.

It's time to look around, see the landscape, and understand that fighting for homeownership isn't just a personal goal; it's part of a larger struggle for independence and fairness. Every one of us who steps onto the homeownership ladder, who chooses to build equity and invest in our own futures, weakens the stranglehold of a system that would rather see us pay rent for life. This is your chance to carve out a piece of the future, to build a foundation that doesn't shift every time a landlord decides to cash in or an investor buys up more of the neighborhood.

So, light the fire and take control. Homeownership isn't just about having a place to call your own—it's about pushing back against a system that profits off your need to belong. It's a declaration of independence, a way to reclaim your future from the endless grind of rent payments and rising costs. Own your home, own your future, and make it clear that you won't be just another cog in a machine built for someone else's benefit. This is your life, your wealth, your chance. Make it count.

Chapter 8:

The Fight for Accessible Homeownership: Reclaiming the American Dream

Owning a home might sound like the "American Dream"—that shiny goal we're all supposed to reach if we just work hard enough, save enough, and maybe skip enough lattes. But let's face it, the game has changed, and the deck is stacked. These days, trying to buy a home feels less like a dream and more like trying to infiltrate an exclusive club where the bouncers are your student loans, rising rents, and that corporate landlord who hikes up the rent every year. When you make the choice to own, you're not just signing up for a mortgage; you're challenging a system that thrives on keeping you renting, dependent, and on the outside looking in.

In the world we're living in, paying rent has become a kind of subscription service—one where you never actually get to own anything. Every month, you're signing up to pay for something you'll never keep. And the kicker? It's someone else's mortgage you're paying off. Rent is the ultimate loyalty program, except there are no points, no perks, just the bleak satisfaction of knowing you're building someone else's equity while yours remains a ghostly "what if."

Homeownership isn't just about four walls and a roof. It's about cutting the puppet strings that keep you dancing to someone else's financial tune. Buying a home is a form of quiet rebellion against a system that wants you docile, obedient, and dependent. It's a way of saying, "Enough. I'm done funding your empire while scrambling to save whatever pennies you leave me." And it's about time more people wake up to that reality. Because in a world where homeownership is slipping further out of reach, deciding to own is more than just a financial decision—it's a rallying cry, a personal protest, and a rejection of the system that would rather see you locked in the renter's cycle, forever footing the bill for someone else's future.

Let me tell you about Emily—a single mother of two from Ohio, working as a nurse, often pulling double shifts just to keep her family afloat. For years, she lived in a small, drafty apartment in a neighborhood where rents kept climbing, eating into her already-stretched budget. Every paycheck seemed to slip through her fingers, no matter how many corners she cut, and every month's rent felt like pouring water into a bucket with a hole at the bottom. As Emily put it, 'I was paying more each month, but it was like my future kept getting smaller.'

Emily knew that homeownership could be her way out. But between her student loans and rising living costs, saving for a down payment felt like an impossible dream. The thought of buying a house in her area was daunting—especially with lenders telling her that without a 20% down payment, she'd be paying higher rates and monthly private mortgage insurance. She'd stare at the mortgage calculators online, the numbers mocking her effort to break free from the rental cycle.

But Emily wasn't the type to back down from a challenge. She'd learned how to face life head-on, balancing work, motherhood, and countless obstacles. So, she started researching every first-time homebuyer program and financial aid option available. Nights that used to be spent unwinding in front of the TV were now filled with endless online searches, figuring out if she qualified for any local or federal down payment assistance. She applied for grants, went to financial workshops, and even joined a community group focused on affordable homeownership—anything that could get her closer to her goal.

It wasn't an easy road. Between the hoops she had to jump through, the waitlists, and the mounds of paperwork, Emily felt like the system was built to make people give up before they even had a chance. 'I had to fight every step of the way,' she recalled. 'It's like they make you prove you're worthy of owning something.' But Emily kept pushing, even when the odds seemed stacked against her.

Finally, after years of grit and determination, Emily pulled together just enough for the down payment on a small, modest home—a place with a leaky roof, creaky floors, and a lawn that had seen better days. To her, it was perfect. The moment she got the keys, she felt something she hadn't felt in a long time: stability. No more moving at the whim of a landlord, no more annual rent hikes. For the first time, Emily could paint the walls any color she wanted, plant a garden in the backyard, and feel a real sense of control over her life.

But the victory went beyond personal pride. Owning that home meant Emily was finally building something for herself and her kids—an asset, a piece of equity, a future. She wasn't just paying for a roof over her head; she was paying into her own wealth, her own legacy. Her monthly payments weren't padding someone else's pocket—they were going toward something she owned, something she could someday pass down to her children. Her kids wouldn't have to grow up moving from apartment to apartment, never knowing what it felt like to have a place that was truly theirs.

Emily's story isn't just one of personal triumph; it's a testament to the quiet, relentless fight people like her endure just to break out of a system built to keep them renting. For her, buying a home wasn't just a financial transaction—it was her declaration of independence, her way of reclaiming a future that the system had almost convinced her wasn't possible. She defied the odds, armed herself with knowledge, and ultimately took back the power that so many renters are denied.

For Emily, homeownership is more than four walls and a roof. It's proof that she wasn't going to let the system decide her family's future. And as she sits on her porch, watching her kids play in the yard, she knows she's won a victory far greater than anyone else can see.

Meet Jonah. A guitarist in a metal band from Minneapolis, where life was loud, raw, and unapologetic—qualities Jonah carried into every part of his life, especially when he picked up his guitar. But his landlord? Let's just say they didn't share Jonah's enthusiasm for thrashing chords and double bass drum riffs. Jonah was constantly reminded that his life didn't fit neatly within the thin walls of his rented apartment.

Every band practice turned into a battle. There'd be a knock on the door, followed by a complaint about "unacceptable sound levels," and eventually fines stacked up like concert posters on his wall. One night, his landlord reached a new level of hostility, calling the police to put a stop to what he called a "public nuisance." For Jonah, it wasn't just irritating; it was a slap in the face. Here he was, paying a small fortune every month to live under someone else's roof, bound by rules that stifled the very thing that defined him. He was investing in his landlord's mortgage, while his dreams and freedom were left at the mercy of someone else's patience.

It was this realization—that his rent payments were only fueling someone else's investment—that hit him like a power chord through a vintage amp. Every dollar he poured into that place gave him nothing in return, except the faint hope that maybe this month, the cops wouldn't show up. Jonah was done. He was done pouring his hard-earned cash and energy into a black hole of rent. He was done tiptoeing around his own life, afraid to live out loud. The only solution? Find a space he could truly call his own.

For Jonah, a musician with a modest income from gigs and a part-time job at a record store, homeownership felt as distant as his childhood rock-star dreams. But he wasn't one to back down. He began researching affordable housing options, even if they were fixer-uppers on the "creative" side of town. He scoured online listings, attended financial literacy workshops, and eventually worked with a first-time homebuyer counselor. His friends teased him, calling his newfound interest in budgeting "unmetal," but Jonah knew this was his way out. Every extra gig, every dollar saved from not buying a new pedal—it all went into his "Freedom Fund."

Months turned into years of scrimping, saving, and grinding. Then, finally,

Jonah found it: a modest house on the outskirts of the city, complete with a dilapidated garage that most people wouldn't look twice at. But to Jonah, it was perfect. It wasn't pristine, but it was his. A place with four walls that he could rattle as loud as he wanted. No noise complaints, no warning letters, and certainly no landlords who could evict him for doing what he loved.

With his bandmates by his side, Jonah transformed the beat-up garage into a sanctuary of sound. They soundproofed the walls, turning it into a haven where his music could thrive. No longer limited by thin walls and curfews, Jonah's music took on a new life. He'd crank his amp, let the distortion sing, and for the first time, he could play without fear of who might be listening in disapproval. That garage wasn't just a practice space; it was his domain—a place he'd affectionately named "Rigby's Dungeon" (a nod to the Regular Show reference that only his bandmates fully appreciated).

Owning this home did more than just give Jonah a place to crank up the volume. It gave him control. He was no longer bound by leases, no longer at the mercy of a landlord's mood swings. Every mortgage payment wasn't just a check disappearing into the ether; it was an investment in his future, a stake in his freedom. And every day he came home, he felt it—that sense of pride and stability, knowing he wasn't just working toward a paycheck but toward something that was truly his.

Today, Rigby's Dungeon isn't just a garage—it's a testament to everything Jonah's fought for. The walls hold the sounds of late-night jam sessions, of riff ideas scratched into notebooks, of dreams built note by note. His house isn't just a shelter; it's a symbol of independence, a hard-won freedom from the rental grind. For Jonah, homeownership wasn't just about finding a place to live. It was about taking control, reclaiming his autonomy, and finally having the space to live unapologetically on his terms.

Jonah's journey shows us that homeownership is more than just financial stability. It's about having a space where you're free to be yourself, with no one dictating the rules. It's about saying, "This is my space, my rules." And for anyone who's ever had to compromise their dreams for the sake of rent, that's worth every single power chord.

Jonah's journey into homeownership was one of rebellion—fueled by the loud, relentless passion of a musician who refused to quiet down. His rented basement apartment was never meant to be a long-term stop, just a cheap place to play until he could afford something better. But the longer he stayed, the clearer it became: as long as he rented, someone else was calling the shots. Every "turn it down" from his landlord was another reminder that no matter how much he paid, he was living on someone else's terms. After the umpteenth noise complaint and the police at his door, he finally had enough. Jonah knew he'd rather pour his energy—and his money—into a place where he could finally play without fear of getting kicked out.

Then there was Emily, a single mother who'd spent years renting in a city that never seemed to welcome her. With each rent increase, each new landlord, she felt the precariousness of her living situation. She'd never missed a rent payment, always kept the place tidy, but it didn't matter—she had no real security. When her building changed hands, and the new landlord decided to "upgrade" the units, she was given a choice: accept a significant rent hike or move out. It was a harsh reminder that renting meant constant vulnerability. It was as if the walls that sheltered her and her son could be pulled away at any moment.

For both Jonah and Emily, homeownership wasn't just a financial decision—it was about taking back control. Jonah wanted a space where he could let his creativity flourish, while Emily craved stability for her family. Each of them found themselves staring down a system that seemed set up to keep people like them in a permanent state of flux. Rent checks, deposits, fines, and late fees—all funneling into someone else's pocket, building someone else's equity, all while they were left with nothing but another month's receipt. Ownership, for them, was a lifeline to something real, something that couldn't be yanked away by someone else's decision.

When Jonah finally signed the papers for his fixer-upper—Rigby's Dungeon, as he called it (a cheeky nod to Regular Show)—it felt like reclaiming more than just a house. It was a declaration: This is mine, my music, my walls, my future. Emily, too, found herself with keys in hand to a modest home on a quiet street, one she could finally make her own without the shadow of a rent increase looming over her. Her son could have a real backyard to play in, walls she could paint any color, a place they could settle into without constantly looking over their shoulders.

Their stories aren't unique, but that's precisely the point. Jonah and Emily are everyday people, each searching for a way out of a cycle that so many find themselves trapped in. And while their journeys to homeownership were very different—one driven by artistic freedom, the other by family stability—they both found something transformative at the end of it. For Jonah, it was the freedom to live his life at full volume. For Emily, it was the peace of knowing her son had a stable roof over his head.

In a world where renting often means staying at the mercy of someone else's decisions, homeownership becomes an act of quiet defiance. It's a way of saying, "I'm done with living on someone else's terms." When we talk about homeownership as empowerment, we're talking about giving people like Jonah and Emily the chance to take back control—not just of where they live, but of their futures.

Jonah and Emily's stories are more than just anecdotes; they're living proof of what ownership can provide beyond a roof and walls. For Jonah, it wasn't just about getting away from noise complaints—it was about finally finding a space where he could exist without constraints, where his music could fill the air without someone else's rules dictating his every move. It was a claim to his own little corner of the world, a place where his art and his life could breathe freely. For Emily, homeownership meant stability after a lifetime of unstable rentals. Her home gave her the first real chance to put down roots, build community, and invest in a future that was finally hers to shape.

These stories illustrate that homeownership isn't just about financial equity—it's about personal equity. When you own a home, it's not only an investment in the real estate market but an investment in your life and dreams. It's where you decide the rules, the decor, the noise levels. In a rental, there's always the feeling of impermanence, as if you're living on borrowed time. But in a home you own, every corner, every wall, is yours. You're not just another tenant; you're the one at the helm.

And while not everyone wants or needs to be a homeowner, the choice to be one—or the option to try—should be within reach. Jonah's freedom to create music in his own space, and Emily's peace of mind in having a place to truly call her own, aren't privileges; they're the kinds of life-building opportunities that shouldn't be reserved only for those who can afford soaring down payments or navigate the byzantine mortgage world. It's about having the option to build something that's lasting, something that stands as both a financial foundation and a personal sanctuary.

These lessons stretch beyond individual ownership, too. When multiplied across neighborhoods, they ripple out into communities, creating a stable foundation for collective growth. Homeownership fosters commitment to local schools, infrastructure, and businesses. It cultivates neighborhoods where people are invested in their surroundings, where they aren't just passersby in a rental cycle but stakeholders in a shared future.

In a world where housing insecurity and rental costs keep people on edge, ownership offers something invaluable: stability. It's a form of personal empowerment that gives people agency in their own lives, allowing them to make choices that align with their values and aspirations. The journey might be challenging, but the impact—on individuals, on communities, on society—is undeniable.

Jonah and Emily's paths to homeownership are stories of personal victories, but they represent something bigger. Each home purchased, each mortgage signed, is a quiet step in a larger movement. Their journeys aren't just about escaping rent or finding a permanent address—they're about reclaiming autonomy in a system that often feels rigged to keep people dependent. And when multiplied across communities, these individual acts of ownership create a collective resilience that strengthens neighborhoods, cities, and even generations.

When people like Jonah and Emily shift from renting to owning, they're not just trading leases for mortgages. They're investing in their communities in a way that renters often can't. Homeowners are more likely to become involved in local schools, attend city council meetings, support neighborhood businesses, and vote on policies that affect their area. It's a ripple effect: each person who gains a foothold in homeownership brings stability to their family and, in doing so, to the community around them. This commitment to place—the sense that you're no longer just passing through—builds neighborhoods that are stronger, safer, and more vibrant.

But there's another side to this, too. When homeownership remains out of reach, the effects spread just as widely. Communities with high rates of renting often lack the same stability. People come and go, landlords change, rents rise and fall. The constant churn undermines the sense of rootedness that makes a community thrive.

Schools lose families, businesses lose regular customers, and local issues can feel like someone else's problem when there's no ownership to tie people to a place. In this way, housing accessibility isn't just a personal issue—it's a public one, affecting the health of communities and the people within them.

And let's be clear: homeownership alone isn't a silver bullet. Jonah's story might end in Rigby's Dungeon, but it took grit, sacrifice, and a system that worked against him at every turn. Emily's peace was hard-won, a result of years battling through financial strains and the stress of relocations. For every success story, there are countless others still searching for stability in a landscape that feels designed to keep it just out of reach. But every story like Jonah's and Emily's gives others a glimpse of what's possible, sparking the kind of hope that moves people to action—whether it's finding a way to buy, advocating for change, or simply realizing that they're not alone in the struggle.

As more people embrace the journey to ownership, the impact grows. It's not just about the individual—each person who gains that foothold helps tip the scales toward a future where homeownership isn't a rare privilege, but an attainable right. The more homeowners there are, the louder the collective voice becomes, demanding policies that support affordable housing, fair lending, and community investment.

Jonah and Emily's stories serve as blueprints for the future. They show us that, yes, the path is tough, and the obstacles are real. But their victories remind us that the fight for accessible homeownership is worth it—not just for personal freedom, but for the future of entire communities. By standing up to a system that profits from keeping people locked in cycles of dependency, each new homeowner takes a small but powerful step toward a more equitable world, where everyone has the opportunity to lay down roots, build wealth, and define their own space.

When we talk about owning a home, we're not just talking about buying a building. We're talking about claiming a space where your choices are yours—free from the hovering control of a landlord or the constant threat of rent hikes. For Jonah, buying that modest house with the rundown garage wasn't just a step toward financial independence; it was his way of breaking free from what felt like modern-day serfdom. In Rigby's Dungeon, he found the power to live and create without being forced to play by someone else's rules—a reminder of what homeownership truly means when you've spent years watching your freedom shrink within the bounds of a lease.

But the journey to ownership isn't an easy path, and the barriers along the way can feel endless. Like the peasants in Chapter 1, we're often made to feel that ownership is out of reach, something reserved for those at the top while the rest of us are left to "rent" a place in someone else's wealth-building machine. For every success story like Jonah's or Emily's, there are countless others who are stuck—caught in the grind of saving while rents rise, facing credit barriers, or disheartened by the sheer cost of entry. The walls may not be as literal as they were in medieval times, but the barriers are just as real.

The reality is that navigating these obstacles takes more than determination. It takes knowledge, strategy, and often, a community that's ready to share its resources and experiences. Emily found strength in that network—other parents, veterans, people like her who were fighting for the same dream. Together, they shared tips on building credit, finding affordable lenders, and navigating grants or assistance programs. When one of them figured out a way through the system, they'd spread the word, turning each small victory into a communal roadmap. It's a quiet rebellion against a system that thrives on isolation, showing that the journey to ownership doesn't have to be walked alone.

This shared struggle has echoes from centuries ago, when the working class in the Industrial Revolution banded together, finding power in unity as they fought for rights in a system that often treated them as expendable. Today's homeownership movement carries that same spirit. It's about realizing that these barriers—high prices, restrictive lending standards, corporate competition—aren't just personal hurdles but part of a larger pattern that keeps wealth concentrated at the top. The struggle is collective, and every step toward ownership is a step toward breaking down that structure.

But beyond community support, there's a need for tangible tools. Financial literacy—understanding credit, mortgages, and investment—is a weapon in this fight, a way to avoid the traps of debt and dependency that can keep people locked out of ownership. Just like Jonah took the time to attend workshops and build his "Freedom Fund," every step in gaining financial knowledge is a step toward cutting through the red tape designed to intimidate or confuse. It's about understanding the game, arming oneself against a system that banks on people's lack of understanding to keep them renting rather than owning.

Owning a home may start as an individual journey, but as people like Jonah and Emily show, it doesn't end there. Each person who moves from renting to ownership is contributing to a wider effort—a quiet but powerful stand against a system that profits from keeping people boxed in, bound to leases and limited choices. Together, these new homeowners are reshaping the narrative of what's possible, proving that ownership isn't just a dream for the privileged but a right worth fighting for.

Imagine you're a dog, locked in a parked car on a blazing summer day. The sun's beating down, windows rolled up tight, no air, no water in sight. You're panting, desperate, scratching at the glass, but the doors won't budge. That's the rental market today—a sweltering trap, designed to keep you barely hanging on, just surviving. Every month, your hard-earned cash evaporates into someone else's hands, and no matter how much you try to save or plan, the system's built to keep the pressure on, making sure you're always gasping for just a little bit more air, a little bit more freedom that never quite comes.

In this suffocating setup, it's not hard to see why people like Jonah and Emily pushed against the boundaries, desperate for a way out. For Jonah, every rent check felt like another twist of the collar, his landlord's rules tightening with each noise complaint, each "keep it down" warning that stifled his passion and silenced his music. Emily, on the other hand, felt the slow drip of lost hope as she watched her hard work barely cover rent, her dream of stability slipping further away with every new lease. Both of them lived in that hot car, in a system built to drain them without offering a shred of security or space to grow.

What pushed them to finally break free wasn't just the mounting frustration—it was the realization that they had to fight for their own space, a place they could actually own and control. For them, homeownership wasn't just about stability; it was a form of survival, a way to escape the crushing heat of dependency and reclaim their lives.

The reality that Jonah and Emily faced wasn't just their struggle; it's a mirror of what so many endure today, trapped in a system designed to keep them dependent, without a clear way out. Each monthly payment, each strained compromise, was a reminder that they were working to secure someone else's future, not their own. And for what? To be left vulnerable, with no roots, no real foundation, and no shot at lasting security.

This is the wake-up call. If you're feeling the walls close in, if you're seeing your hard work vanish into someone else's bank account, it's time to realize: this isn't just bad luck. It's a setup. The system isn't broken—it's built to function this way, keeping those at the bottom propping up the comfort of those at the top. But here's the truth that the system hopes you'll ignore: there's still a way out. It may not be easy, but the path to homeownership isn't just a step toward financial stability; it's a powerful act of defiance. It's the decision to stop feeding into the cycle of dependency and start building something that's truly yours.

So, wake up. You don't have to live in someone else's hot car, suffocating and waiting for a change that'll never come. The fight for homeownership isn't just personal—it's about reclaiming control, breaking free from a system rigged against you, and taking back your right to a stable, independent future.

Here's section 5 with the expanded focus on homeownership as both resistance and resilience, building on the urgency and empowerment needed for readers to take control of their future:

Owning a home in today's world isn't just about putting down roots—it's an act of quiet rebellion, a personal declaration against a system built to profit from your dependency. Every dollar put toward a mortgage, every hour spent maintaining your own property, is a decision to invest in your freedom. It's choosing to leave the cycle of endlessly paying someone else's bills. It's a subtle, steady way to break free from the expectations society sets, where so many are steered toward lifetime renting with no end in sight. With each step, you're not just taking control—you're taking a stand.

Think of the current housing market as a carefully orchestrated trap. The system thrives on you staying in your place, paying rent, building wealth for someone else, with the promise that one day, maybe, you'll earn enough to buy your own. But the truth? That "someday" only happens if you make it happen. Homeownership flips the script. When you buy a home, you're no longer a participant in someone else's wealth-building scheme; you're the architect of your own. Every mortgage payment builds equity in something real and lasting, a financial asset that is yours. It's no longer about making ends meet; it's about building something for yourself and your family.

The impact of owning property goes beyond monthly payments and mortgage rates. Homeownership gives you the stability to plan your future without fearing sudden rent hikes, forced relocations, or unexpected changes to your living situation. No landlord's decisions can threaten your stability or uproot your life. That kind of security? It's more than a comfort; it's a foundation to build your life on, the power to make long-term plans, to invest in yourself and your community, and to live on your terms.

And there's a legacy in this autonomy. The difference between renting and owning isn't just measured in dollars; it's in the ability to pass down something of value. With homeownership, you're not just securing your present—you're creating a future that holds meaning and value for generations. The house you buy today isn't just a place to live; it's a symbol of your hard-won independence, a piece of stability that you can leave behind. Every bit of effort and investment becomes a legacy, a gift of security for those who come after you.

This isn't about just affording a mortgage. It's about seizing a rare chance to change the rules. Each person who fights for ownership, who resists the system that says you must be dependent, is part of a broader shift. Collectively, these individual choices form a wave, challenging a society where only a privileged few hold the reins. Homeownership isn't just an economic achievement; it's a social statement. It says that you're not willing to play by the rules of a game designed to keep you boxed in.

But time is a factor. Every year that passes, every policy that favors investors over individual buyers, every corporate buyout of single-family homes narrows the window of opportunity. If we don't act, the doors to ownership will continue to close for those who haven't yet secured a stake. The urgency is real: the choice to buy a home today is a choice to resist being swept into a future where stability is out of reach, where security is a luxury only a few can afford. Now is the time to recognize the power of ownership and claim your place in it.

Don't let this moment slip by. Homeownership is your chance to rewrite the narrative, to create stability and opportunity, and to contribute to a movement that's quietly pushing back against a world that's happy to keep you dependent. Each mortgage payment, each DIY project, each choice you make in your own home is a brick in the wall of your independence. It's proof that you're taking control, that you're building something that can't be easily taken away.

For too damn long, the American Dream of homeownership has felt like a game designed to keep us out—a rigged race where only the wealthy get a real shot at the prize. The rest of us? We're handed a rental agreement, told to pay up, and keep quiet while someone else's equity grows. But it doesn't have to be that way. We have a choice, and it's time we woke up to it. We can keep throwing our hard-earned money into someone else's pocket, building their legacy while our own futures fade into the background—or we can fight back. We can break this cycle, take control, and stop buying into a system that feeds off keeping us locked out.

Owning a home isn't just a way out; it's a way up. It's a form of quiet rebellion, a punch to the gut of a system that profits from keeping us chained to leases and ever-rising rents. By choosing homeownership, we're not just buying a house—we're buying freedom, control, and the right to decide what our lives look like. And this is our moment. We're staring down a closing window of opportunity, where every year that passes, every policy that favors corporate investors over individuals, shrinks the chance for people like us to stake our claim. The choice to buy a home today isn't just about where you live tomorrow—it's about resisting a future where security is a luxury reserved for a select few.

Let's make this clear: Homeownership isn't some distant dream or unattainable luxury. It's our right. Every mortgage payment, every bit of sweat equity poured into our own walls is a step away from a life of dependency and toward a future we actually control. We're building something real—stability, wealth, a legacy that can't be bought and sold by landlords and investors. This is our chance to stand up and say, 'I'm done being a pawn in someone else's game. I'm building something that's mine.'

The path is there. The power is ours. So let's reclaim the American Dream, not just for ourselves, but for everyone who's been told they don't belong in the club. Let's make this stand, flip the script, and create a future where homeownership is a right, not a privilege. This is more than a choice—it's a declaration. Let's take back what's ours.

Chapter 9:

The Cheese Out of the Trap

Let's be clear: the journey to owning a home isn't some leisurely Sunday drive. Picture it more like a marathon on broken pavement, with obstacles thrown at you from every direction. The banks, the market, the gatekeepers—they're all there, like a race designed to see who quits first. But here's the thing: the finish line isn't a luxury; it's your right. If you're tired of being stuck in place while someone else cashes in on your hard work, this is the moment to fight back. Homeownership is the only way to stop paying rent to keep someone else comfortable and start investing in yourself, in your future.

Every rent payment you make is like pouring water into a cup with a hole at the bottom. Month after month, your hard-earned money slips through, filling someone else's pockets while you're left dry. It's not a mistake; it's how the system was built—to keep you on the hook, feeding the wealth of someone else. It's a cycle as ancient as the feudal system, where serfs worked the land and landlords reaped the profits. Fast-forward a few centuries, and here we are, stuck in a modern version of that same trap. If you want a way out, it's going to take grit and commitment, and it starts with choosing to own something for yourself.

Imagine living in a house where every wall, every floorboard, every nail holds the weight of your future. That's the power of ownership. It's more than a roof over your head; it's freedom from the endless loop of rent payments and eviction notices, where someone else decides your fate. In your own home, you're the one with control. There's no landlord looming, no unexpected rent hikes, no notice-to-vacate because they decided to remodel. When you own, you're not just securing a place to live—you're claiming your independence from a system that's designed to keep you on the hook forever.

But here's the kicker: this isn't a journey that comes easily. There will be days when the numbers don't add up, when the market seems rigged, and when every step forward feels like two steps back. The people who benefit from keeping you renting will make sure of that. They're the ones who profit from high rents, from restricted inventory, from the fact that you can't save for a down payment because all your income goes toward their profits. It's a game, and the rules are rigged. But there's one thing they can't control—your decision to start moving forward. Owning a home is about rewriting those rules, carving your own path out of the maze they've set up.

Think of every barrier they throw at you as a test—a test of how badly you want it, of how willing you are to take back control of your life. They'll try to make it hard, but every sacrifice, every extra shift worked, every dollar saved, brings you closer. For every person who fights through, who refuses to give up, there's a ripple that reaches farther than just one household. It's about creating a movement, about proving that homeownership isn't just for the privileged few at the top of the ladder.

It's a quiet, powerful protest, a way of taking a stand against a system that banks on your dependency.

In the end, every single mortgage payment isn't just a step toward stability; it's a defiant middle finger to a system that hoped you'd settle for less. It's about more than numbers; it's about freedom, about taking ownership of your life and your future. For the first time, the investment is in your name, in something that won't be stripped away by someone else's whims. The mortgage? It's not a chain; it's a foundation. It's a way to own your own slice of security, to build something solid that no one else can take.

This is your journey, your fight. It's not just about breaking free from renting—it's about refusing to let a rigged system define your future. If you're ready to take that first step, then you're already part of something bigger than yourself. This isn't just about owning a home. It's about reclaiming the right to stability, control, and a future that's truly yours.

Here's the harsh truth: as long as you're renting, you're fueling someone else's future, not your own. Imagine it like clockwork, every single month—your hard-earned money goes into someone else's pocket, building their wealth, while you're left right where you started. It's a cycle of dependency, and it's designed to keep you feeling like homeownership is just a fantasy, something other people do. The goal of the system? To make you forget that ownership is even an option. To keep you stuck, paying someone else's mortgage instead of building a future for yourself.

Think of every rent check as a brick in the wall that's been built to keep you in place. It's a subtle trap, really—a lifetime subscription to someone else's financial security. Meanwhile, your own dreams of stability, of financial freedom, are set aside as you're told, month after month, that this is just the way things are. They want you comfortable in that cycle, willing to accept that this is all there is. It's like a never-ending treadmill, one where you keep moving but never actually go anywhere.

But what if you could break that cycle? What if, instead of handing over your paycheck to someone else, you used it to build something that was truly yours? That's the power of homeownership. It's not just about having a roof over your head—it's about stepping off the treadmill and finally going somewhere. Every mortgage payment is a building block, stacking up equity and stability. With each dollar, you're saying, "This is mine. This is my future, and no one else's." It's about taking back the control that the rental market has tried to strip away from you.

The first step? Realize that the walls around you aren't as solid as they seem. Yes, the market is tough. Yes, the system is rigged. But every time you work toward ownership, every step you take to save, to build credit, to plan for your future, you're chipping away at those walls. You're proving that you won't be confined by a system that profits from keeping you boxed in. The decision to pursue homeownership is a decision to reclaim your future—one step, one payment, one plan at a time.

And let's be real: the system doesn't want you to break free. There are entire industries that thrive on the rental cycle, on the churn of tenants who move in, pay up, and move out. They bank on the fact that you'll stay in their web of endless payments. But the moment you decide that ownership is the goal, you're putting up a fight. You're saying that you're done settling for a financial plan that only benefits someone else. And that shift—from accepting to challenging—is the most powerful move you can make.

When you own, you're no longer at the mercy of landlords who can raise the rent on a whim or evict you when it suits their plans. You're the one in control. You're the one who decides where to invest, what improvements to make, how to build your space. You're no longer paying for someone else's retirement fund; you're building your own. It's a transition from paying for a place to stay, to investing in a place to live—a place that's truly yours, a place that grows with you.

This journey isn't about a single victory; it's about a series of small wins, each one a step closer to ownership and independence. Every dollar saved, every budget cut, every bit of financial discipline—it's all a part of the process of breaking free. It's about refusing to let the system dictate your life and instead taking ownership of your own path. It's about standing up and saying that your future isn't just an expense—it's an investment worth every bit of effort you put in.

So, if you're ready to escape the cycle, know this: you're not alone, and the walls aren't impenetrable. The system banks on you staying dependent, but the moment you take that first step toward ownership, you're shaking its foundation. You're building something that's truly yours, and with every step, you're gaining ground. Homeownership isn't just a financial milestone; it's a declaration of independence, a way of breaking free from a cycle that was never meant to serve you. Take the first step, and you're already halfway out of the trap.

Imagine life as a puppet show, where invisible strings pull you every which way—where you move, how much you pay, even how much of your paycheck goes into someone else's hands. For renters, that's not far from reality. You're in a system where someone else calls the shots, where each rent check is a reminder that you're building someone else's empire while you stay right where they want you—on the outside, looking in. But here's the truth they don't want you to know: there's a way to cut those strings. It's not easy, but it starts with one thing they can't take from you—knowledge.

Financial literacy isn't just about "being smart with money" or knowing how to balance a checkbook. It's the flashlight in a dark, winding maze, showing you the cracks and openings in a system that profits from your dependency. It's knowing how credit works, understanding the fine print of a mortgage, seeing the difference between an "affordable" payment and a lifetime of debt. The more you know, the less power the system has over you. With every piece of knowledge, you're loosening the grip they have, making it harder for anyone to take advantage of you. You're not just learning; you're arming yourself.

For too long, financial tools have been hidden behind walls of jargon and gatekeeping. But by taking control of this knowledge—by learning the ins and outs of credit, budgeting, and home loans—you're stepping into a role you've been kept out of: the owner. Ownership isn't just a financial step; it's a shift in power. It's moving from a place where you're at someone else's mercy to a place where you're in control. Imagine a life without rent hikes, without eviction threats, without that nagging uncertainty every time a lease renewal rolls around. Ownership puts the power back in your hands, making you the architect of your own future.

But let's not sugarcoat it: the path to ownership isn't a walk in the park. The system is rigged, designed to keep you renting, dependent, with each year feeling more like an endless loop. Your rent payments don't build equity; they build someone else's fortune. Every dollar you spend is another brick in their empire, while you're left in a cycle that drains your resources without giving anything back. That's why ownership isn't just about stability; it's a rebellion. It's a choice to stop pouring your energy into someone else's pockets and start building something real for yourself.

Think of ownership as the ultimate act of defiance in a game designed to keep you losing. With each step toward homeownership, you're saying, "I'm done playing by your rules." Financial literacy gives you the tools, but ownership gives you the foundation to stand on. You're no longer a cog in the rental machine, no longer paying for someone else's luxuries while you scrape by. When you own, you're investing in yourself, building equity that belongs to you, creating a legacy that's yours alone. It's about making your money work for you—not for some landlord's next vacation home.

And the impact doesn't stop at your front door. Ownership isn't just about personal stability; it's about community. When you buy, you're not just putting down roots for yourself. You're investing in a neighborhood, supporting local businesses, and creating a ripple effect that strengthens entire communities. Imagine if more people could break free from the rental cycle—if more of us could stake our claims and build wealth that lasts. The power would shift. It would change neighborhoods, cities, and maybe even the balance of who holds real power in society. Ownership isn't just personal; it's collective resilience.

This is what they don't want you to realize. Every time you gain control over your finances, every step you take toward homeownership, you're pushing back against a system that thrives on your dependency. Financial literacy is your shield, ownership your sword. Together, they cut through the illusion that renting forever is your only option. By owning, you're not just securing your future—you're taking a stand. You're reclaiming your life from a system that profits off keeping you in place, boxed in by limitations they set. And in that quiet act of rebellion, you're building more than just wealth. You're building freedom, stability, and a legacy that no one else controls.

So, when you think about buying a home, don't just see it as "the next step." See it for what it really is: the power to decide your own future, to live without strings attached, to stand on your own terms. Financial literacy and ownership are the keys to a life where you're no longer paying for someone else's dreams—you're finally investing in your own.

Picture this: a neighborhood where people know each other by name, where they aren't just passing through but are invested in each other's lives, in the local schools, in the parks, and in the businesses down the street. Now imagine a different reality—a row of rental units, where people come and go, each new tenant a stranger, each departure leaving the place a little emptier. That's the difference ownership brings. It's not just about stability; it's about the transformation of entire communities. When people own, they aren't just investing in four walls and a roof—they're putting down roots, shaping the very fabric of a neighborhood.

The beauty of homeownership lies in this ripple effect. When someone like you decides to buy, you're not only gaining a piece of property—you're building a foundation that supports everyone around you. With each mortgage payment, you're fueling a local economy that thrives on small businesses, local jobs, and community growth. When you own, you're not just another transient tenant. You become a stakeholder, a contributor to something larger than yourself. That sense of permanence, that feeling that you have a say in the place you live? It's a quiet revolution, one household at a time.

But the system doesn't make this easy. It would rather keep neighborhoods transient, shifting, and full of renters who are here today, gone tomorrow. Because here's the thing about renters: they're often disconnected. It's hard to feel invested in a community when you're constantly worried about rent hikes, when you know that next year, or even next month, you might have to pack up and move again. The system counts on this—it thrives on communities without roots, where the only stability is found in corporate landlords who call the shots from miles away. Ownership, on the other hand, disrupts this model. It creates communities where people care, where the collective strength is built on shared investment, where the power lies not with distant landlords but with the people who actually live there.

When people buy homes, they take ownership of more than just their property; they take ownership of their surroundings. They're more likely to attend local meetings, support neighborhood businesses, and advocate for the changes they want to see. Think about it: if you're paying someone else's mortgage, your involvement is often limited by your temporary stake in the area. But when you own? You're invested in the long game. You're contributing to something that's yours, something that can grow in value, both economically and socially. Ownership fosters accountability, not just to the house you live in but to the larger community that surrounds it.

Homeownership brings power back to the people—something the system would rather keep out of reach. It's a collective power, where individuals become part of a community network. This isn't just some feel-good notion; it's a fundamental shift in who holds control. When communities are full of owners rather than tenants, they're harder to displace, harder to gentrify without resistance. It's a way of saying, "This is ours, and we have a stake in what happens here." Ownership creates resilience, a buffer against the constant upheavals that rental cycles bring. And that resilience? It builds communities that don't just survive; they thrive.

Think of homeownership as a subtle but powerful form of social currency. When you own, your voice carries more weight, your opinions are taken more seriously, and your presence matters. That's because ownership isn't just about financial stability; it's about belonging. It's about walking through your neighborhood with the knowledge that you're not just another face in a temporary crowd. You're part of a legacy, a chain of owners who've built, invested, and strengthened the very place you call home.

But let's be real: the system doesn't want this kind of solidarity. It doesn't want neighborhoods that push back, that have the power to say "no" to destructive developments, that rally together for shared causes. A neighborhood of renters is easier to manipulate, to shift, to exploit. Homeowners, on the other hand, are far more likely to resist, to demand a say in what goes on. Ownership isn't just about individual freedom; it's about collective strength, the ability to defend your community against forces that would strip it of its character, its stability, its future.

And this is why homeownership is so much more than a personal goal. It's a fundamental building block of a society where people have a voice, a place, and a power that's rooted in something real. Each home bought is a quiet act of resistance, a claim that "we belong here, too." Ownership creates lasting change, not only for you but for the neighbors who walk beside you, the local businesses you support, and the schools your children attend. It's a movement of people taking back control, one property, one street, one community at a time.

So, as you think about homeownership, remember: it's not just about you. It's about the community you'll be part of, the legacy you'll leave, the strength you'll bring to a neighborhood that needs people who care. Ownership is more than a financial decision; it's an investment in a future where communities are built on the backs of those who live, love, and labor within them—not on the whims of distant landlords who see only dollar signs. Each new homeowner strengthens this silent revolution, shifting the balance of power, grounding communities in something more enduring than leases and monthly checks.

Homeownership isn't just a financial journey; it's an exercise in grit, endurance, and sheer willpower. This path might test you more than you ever expected, throwing obstacles your way just when you feel like you're making progress. But here's the truth: every challenge, every setback, every delay is part of a process that will make the end result even more meaningful. When you finally hold the keys to a place that's yours, you'll know that you earned every inch of that freedom.

When the world tells you that owning a home is out of reach, remember that you're not alone in this fight. You're part of a generation, a movement, a collective refusal to let this system decide who deserves a stable future and who doesn't. Think of each small step forward—whether it's building your credit score by a few points, setting aside savings each month, or simply educating yourself about the market—as a strike against the idea that only a select few are meant to own. Each choice you make strengthens the foundation beneath your feet.

Yes, there will be days that feel discouraging. Days where saving seems pointless, where you feel like you're working twice as hard just to stay in place. On those days, remind yourself why you started. Remind yourself that this isn't just about owning four walls and a roof. It's about staking a claim to your own future, investing in a vision of life where you're not at the mercy of a landlord, where you're building something that's lasting, stable, and fully yours.

Every journey has hurdles, and this one's no exception. But there's a reason we've covered financial literacy, budgeting, strategic sacrifice, and practical steps—because each one of those is a tool in your arsenal. They're not just ways to get by; they're ways to actively work toward your goal, no matter how distant it may feel. Persistence isn't about never faltering—it's about standing up each time you're knocked back, adjusting your plan as needed, and keeping your eyes firmly on what lies ahead.

And think about the legacy you're building. Imagine the impact that homeownership will have, not only on your life but on those around you—your family, your community, your friends who see what's possible through your example. You're creating a future that doesn't just lift you up but has the potential to inspire others to follow suit. Every person who crosses that finish line, who beats the odds and secures their own home, paves the way for others to do the same.

So when the going gets tough, when the setbacks seem overwhelming, remember: persistence is your greatest tool. Ownership is worth every challenge, every adjustment, every difficult choice. The road might be winding, but it's a road that's worth taking, with rewards that reach far beyond the walls of any single home. This journey, with all its twists and turns, is setting you up not just for homeownership but for a life built on the foundation of your own resilience, strength, and unshakable resolve.

And if you ever doubt that this goal is achievable, remember this: every homeowner who came before you faced obstacles just like yours. They fought, they saved, they sacrificed, and they made it. You're on the same path. You're just as capable. And the reward waiting for you on the other side—a home, a future, and a life you can call your own—is worth every step.

Conclusion

Your Path to Homeownership Starts Here

So here we are, at the end of a book, but the beginning of a journey. Homeownership, as we've explored, is more than just buying a place to live. It's about carving out a space that's truly yours—a piece of independence, stability, and power in a world that all too often tries to keep it out of reach. And now, the steps are yours to take.

Here's your guide to making homeownership a reality. It's not a silver bullet or a shortcut—there are none. It's a realistic plan, grounded in small, steady steps, designed to help you build toward the life you deserve.

Step 1: Set Your Goals and Know Your "Why"

- Define your purpose: Write down why homeownership matters to you. Is it stability? A legacy? Freedom? Your personal "why" is your driving force, and you'll need to hold onto it during the more challenging parts of this journey.
- Visualize your future: Picture yourself in your own home. What does it look like? How does it feel? Let this

image guide you, serving as a reminder of why you're fighting for ownership.

Step 2: Take Control of Your Finances

• Start a budget: Track your income, spending, and savings. Break down your expenses to see where you can save. Even small changes can add up.
• Focus on your credit score: Get a copy of your credit report, review it for errors, and create a plan to improve your score. Pay down debt, make payments on time, and avoid opening unnecessary credit accounts.
• Save consistently: Open a separate account for your homeownership fund and automate monthly transfers, even if they're small.

Consistency is key here; each deposit brings you closer to your goal.

Step 3: Educate Yourself on Homeownership Programs and Financial Options

• Explore assistance programs: Look into federal, state, and local programs designed for first-time homebuyers. Research grants, down payment assistance, and low-interest loans that could help you.
• Attend workshops or counseling sessions: Many community organizations offer free or affordable financial literacy programs, credit counseling, and homebuyer education. These sessions can provide you with the practical knowledge to make informed decisions.

Step 4: Make Strategic Sacrifices

- Identify areas to cut back: This might mean choosing fewer luxuries or making sacrifices in the short term. Find what you can live without and redirect that money into your homeownership fund.
- Consider additional income streams: Part-time work, freelancing, or selling items you no longer need can bring in extra funds. Remember, every dollar saved or earned brings you closer to that down payment.

Step 5: Connect with Community and Mentors

- Find others on the same path: Join local or online groups of first-time buyers to share tips and strategies. A supportive community can make the journey feel less isolating and help you stay motivated.

• Seek mentorship: If possible, connect with people who have been through the process. Their insights can help you navigate challenges, avoid pitfalls, and stay on track.

Step 6: Navigate the Buying Process with Confidence

• Get pre-approved: When you're financially ready, start by getting pre-approved for a mortgage. This shows sellers you're serious and gives you a clear budget.

- Find a knowledgeable real estate agent: Look for someone experienced with first-time buyers who understands your goals. A good agent will help you find options that align with your budget and vision.
- Stay patient and persistent: The housing market can be unpredictable. It may take time to find the right home at the right price, so keep searching and stay focused.

Step 7: Take Ownership—and Don't Look Back

- Make your house a home: Whether it's decorating, renovating, or simply settling in, make the space truly yours. Every choice is a reflection of your journey and the effort it took to get here.

- Celebrate your success: You've achieved something significant—recognize and honor it. Homeownership is more than a purchase; it's a step toward a life where you control your own future.

This journey won't be easy, and the road might feel endless at times. But every challenge you overcome is a step toward freedom from the rental cycle, a step closer to a life where you have control over your own space, and a step toward securing something lasting for yourself and those you care about. The power of homeownership is within your reach. Now, it's up to you to grab it, hold on, and make it yours.

The fight for homeownership is the fight for your future. Let this guide be your map, your reminder, and your rallying call. The dream is real, the work is hard, but the reward? A life built on your terms—where every wall, every floor, and every inch is truly yours. Now go, take that first step, and don't look back.

About the Author

Hey there, I'm Brenton Mann. I'm a U.S. Navy veteran, Realtor. My journey into real estate wasn't just about selling homes; it was about flipping the script on a system that keeps too many people in the endless cycle of rent payments and "maybe one day" dreams. I've made it my mission to help people, especially veterans and first-time buyers, claim their own little corner of the world—without all the fine print and financial traps that seem to come with it.

My story starts with a few deployments and a little place called TOPGUN. Yes, that TOPGUN. I spent years as an aviation electrician with the EA-18G Growler community at Whidbey Island. Let's just say if it flies and has wires, I was probably up to my elbows in it, whether that was during missions in Northern Japan, Okinawa, or joint operations with the Marines in Miramar. And yeah, working at TOPGUN comes with the occasional "I feel the need, the need for speed" moment. But mostly, it taught me grit, patience, and how to tackle problems head-on—which, believe me, is just as useful when dealing with a tricky mortgage.

After the Navy, I wanted to put that same drive into something that actually helps people feel secure—financially, emotionally, you name it. That's where real estate came in. It didn't take long to realize that buying a home was a maze, especially if you don't have a trust fund waiting in the wings. So I decided to focus on veterans and folks facing those same uphill battles. Navigating the world of homeownership shouldn't feel like you're hacking into a government mainframe, yet somehow, it does. I'm here to make sure it doesn't.

I specialize in helping people who are often overlooked by the system. My approach is simple: give people the tools, show them the shortcuts, and maybe crack a few jokes along the way. Owning a home isn't just about picking a place with a nice backyard. It's about stepping off the endless treadmill of rent and saying, "Hey, I'm building something for me and mine." And it's more than a transaction. It's a way of breaking out of the dependency cycle that so many of us have been sold as "normal."

In my off-hours, you'll likely find me in Las Vegas, cooking up something adventurous in the kitchen or spending quality time with my family. Food and family are central to me, and I've always believed that just like a good meal, homeownership has the power to bring people together. It's something satisfying, something you can pour yourself into, and done right, it's something that just feels good.

I've earned several certifications that reflect my commitment to providing specialized, knowledgeable, and inclusive service to my clients, particularly those in unique situations such as military personnel, diverse communities, and those in need of strategic problem-solving. Here's a breakdown of my certifications and what they bring to the table:

Military on the Move Expert: As a Navy veteran myself, I understand the challenges and nuances that military families face when moving—whether it's PCS orders, finding housing in a new location, or navigating the complexities of military benefits. This certification allows me to serve military clients with the expertise they need, ensuring smooth transitions, efficient moves, and access to the right resources.

At Home With Diversity Expert: Homeownership should be a right for everyone, no matter their background. This certification emphasizes my dedication to creating a welcoming and inclusive environment for all buyers, regardless of race, ethnicity, or socioeconomic status. It ensures that

I'm prepared to handle diverse real estate needs and help everyone find a place to call home.

Alliance Certified Ally: This certification reflects my ongoing commitment to advocating for marginalized communities, providing a safe, supportive space where individuals can navigate the homebuying process with confidence. It's about building bridges, fostering inclusivity, and ensuring that no one is left out of the conversation.

Military Relocation Professional (MRP): Military families deserve specialized support during relocations, and this certification enables me to offer tailored services to service members and their families. From understanding

VA loan benefits to managing tight timelines, I have the tools to make military moves as seamless as possible, allowing families to focus on their next chapter rather than the stresses of relocation.

Six Sigma Greenbelt: Process improvement is key to any successful business, and my Six Sigma Greenbelt certification allows me to streamline operations, reduce waste, and improve service quality. This skill ensures that my clients receive not only excellent customer service but an efficient, well-organized real estate experience.

Scrum Master: Real estate transactions often involve multiple parties and fast-paced decision-making. My Scrum Master certification equips me with the skills to lead and manage teams, ensuring that communication, collaboration, and problem-solving are done efficiently. This allows me to provide a smooth process for my clients, ensuring that all aspects of their transaction are handled with precision.

These certifications are more than just letters on my resume—they're a testament to my dedication to providing specialized, efficient, and inclusive service to my clients. Whether it's guiding military families through their move, fostering a diverse client base, or using process improvement techniques to deliver a seamless experience, I'm here to make homeownership accessible and successful for everyone.

Beyond my work as a Realtor, I'm deeply committed to the community here in Las Vegas. I'm actively involved with organizations like Crisis Text Line, Pop Warner Youth Football, Harvison House, and USVets, dedicating my time to causes that align with my values. I also advocate for environmental preservation, working to keep our neighborhoods and natural spaces beautiful and thriving. For me, community isn't just where we live; it's the people and the places that shape us, and I'm honored to give back in ways that matter.

One of my greatest passions is teaching veteran homebuying classes. As a Navy veteran myself, I understand the unique challenges veterans face when it comes to securing stable housing. These classes aren't just about buying a house—they're about empowering my fellow veterans with the knowledge and tools to achieve financial independence. It's a chance to bridge the knowledge gap, ensuring that more veterans can plant roots, grow their own wealth, and create a lasting legacy for their families. I believe homeownership is a lot like a good meal: it's satisfying, it brings people together, and, done right, it just feels good. At the end of the day, it's about giving people the chance to plant roots, grow their own wealth, and—let's be honest—finally paint the walls whatever color they want.

The information shared in this book is meant for general informational purposes only. While the experiences and insights I share reflect my journey and passion for real estate, financial literacy, and homeownership, they are not intended as professional legal, financial, or real estate advice. Every individual's situation is unique, so if you're making decisions about finances, mortgages, or real estate, I highly recommend consulting with a qualified professional who can guide you based on your personal circumstances.

This book does not replace expert advice. If you're looking for specific guidance in these areas, whether it's about buying a home or navigating finances, please consult with a certified financial planner, a real estate agent licensed in your state, or a legal professional. You should always make decisions based on your personal needs, resources, and goals.

Just as every homebuyer's path is different, the results from applying the strategies and advice in this book may vary. I can't guarantee success, and the information shared here is based on my personal experiences. I've had my own successes, but your journey might take a different path—and that's okay! What matters is you're starting it.

Ultimately, the goal here is to empower you with the tools and insights to help you take control of your homeownership journey. But remember, what worked for me or others might not be a one-size-fits-all solution. Take what resonates, and always make decisions that are right for you!

www.ingramcontent.com/pod-product-compliance
Lightning Source LLC
Chambersburg PA
CBHW032211220526
45472CB00018B/668